Everything You Need To Know About Estate Planning In Illinois

By Denice Gierach

This book was written as a public service by Denice A. Gierach of The Gierach Law Firm. While the information provided relates to legal issues, it is not legal advice or legal representation. Because of the rapidly changing nature of the law, the author makes no warranty or guarantee of the accuracy or reliability of information contained herein. Every individual's situation is unique and requires different strategies and tactics for maximum benefit. Therefore, we recommend calling The Gierach Law Firm at 630-756-1160 to have a personal, confidential conversation about your specific needs and goals.

Introduction

I've been providing comprehensive estate planning for over 30 years, and I've found that my clients have a lot of the same questions and concerns.

There are many complex aspects to putting together an effective estate plan, and often, people don't even know what questions they should ask.

That's why I wrote this book—because I'm betting that you have many of those same questions.

I've included some of those important questions, and their answers, as well as other important issues and general information in this book. I hope you find this helpful.

You work hard all your life for your money, and it's my job to help make sure that you keep as much of it as possible during your lifetime, and that as much of it as possible goes to the people you choose upon your death with speed and ease.

-Denice

Table of Contents

Appendix 217

Part I:

Frequently Asked Questions Regarding Estate Planning

1

What is estate planning? What is estate administration?

E state planning is a process, beginning with meeting a professional advisor to organize your assets, assess your wishes, and draft important documents, to ensure that your wealth is distributed as you would like upon your death. The process of estate planning allows you to plan ahead to meet your lifetime objectives, as well as to provide for the disposition of your personal assets at your death.

When most people hear "estate planning," their first thought is drafting a Last Will and Testament as a way to determine how their assets will be transferred to their loved ones upon their death. The core document most often associated with estate planning is a will, but most plans often include other documents, such as a living trust and powers of attorney.

The process of estate planning first requires a fully thought-out plan with a qualified estate planning attorney, coupled with the proper documentation of the plan, using a will, trust, powers of attorney and other estate planning devices that are essential to the services that an estate planning attorney can provide.

Estate administration is the process of handling the estate of a deceased person. It includes collecting assets, making an inventory and appraising those assets, paying and collecting debts, filing and paying estate taxes and income taxes, and distributing the remaining assets to the beneficiaries of the estate. An experienced lawyer can simplify the process for the family of the deceased person.

Estate planning is impacted by changes in federal and state law, particularly the tax and inheritance laws. As a result, you may find that you will require an attorney with a solid background in estate planning and tax law to create a more elaborate legal plan that fits your needs and complies with the federal and state laws. Your attorney is an essential part in assuring that your estate planning goals are properly set and carried out.

2

What is a will?

A will is a written legal document which sets forth instructions for the distributions of a person's assets after his or her death. It is the core document most often associated with estate planning.

Most people are familiar with a Last Will and Testament as a way to ensure property transfers correctly from the deceased to their beneficiaries, but a will can accomplish more than just that.

A will also outlines who will oversee the estate assets by serving as executor, what will be required of the executor, the authority of the executor, and who will be appointed guardian of any minor children, among other things.

Each state has a statute that determines the necessary attributes of a valid will. In Illinois, the will must be in writing, signed by the testator, who is of sound mind and memory at the time of the execution of the will, and the testator's signature must be properly witnessed at the time of the execution of the will, as well.

3

What is considered a part of my estate?

All of the assets you own at the time of your death are considered a part of your estate. This would include both real property and personal property.

Real property is real estate and land that you own, including anything growing on, attached to, or erected on that land, such as your house or crops.

Personal property is any movable or intangible thing that is subject to ownership, such as the things you buy. Some examples include cash, your car, your house, your share in a business, your securities, or your retirement plan, 401(k), IRA, or a life insurance policy.

4

Why do I need estate planning?

For families with substantial assets, particularly those with a family business, the estate planning process offers many options to benefit the family today and in the future.

Many goals can be accomplished through successful estate planning, such as:

- Minimizing taxes today and minimizing estate taxes tomorrow;
- Saving for retirement;
- Funding a child's education;

- Ensuring your minor children, dependent family members, and other loved ones are taken care of, including those who may need financial or other assistance;
- Leaving a charitable legacy and giving back to those causes that you support ;
- Protecting the future of a business.

In addition, estate planning allows you to express your wishes clearly and ensure they are carried out.

5

What benefits does a well-designed estate plan provide me and my family?

A well-designed estate plan can offer you many benefits.

For example, it can:

- Make the administration of your estate simpler and easier on your family when you die;
- Protect you and your heirs in the event that you become incapacitated;
- Allow you to create structure well in advance, instead of leaving it until the last minute or waiting until it is too late;

- Preserve the value of your assets;
- Ensure your intentions regarding what your beneficiaries receive are carried out; and
- Reduce or avoid unnecessary taxes, to the extent allowed by law.

6

What is probate?

P robate is a court process that determines the validity of the will and then causes an orderly administration of the estate.

A legal notice is published for any outstanding claims against your estate and starts a claims period during which claims can be filed. Claims filed after the claims period may be barred.

After taxes, claims of creditors that were allowed and administration fees are paid, the remaining assets of the estate are distributed to the beneficiaries, who are listed in the will. If there is no valid will, the assets are distributed according to the provisions in the state's intestacy statute.

7

What does the probate process include?

T he probate process might include:

- Proving a will is valid;
- Paying outstanding bills and taxes;
- Selling or distributing property to heirs according to terms of the will;
- A third-party mediator to settle disputes;
- Filing court paperwork;
- Preparing the inventory of the estate;
- Obtaining appraisals of property and assets;

- Locating heirs;
- Collecting money owed to the deceased person;
- Filing state and federal income tax returns for the deceased and for the estate;
- Preparing state and federal estate tax returns.

8

What assets are covered by probate? Can I avoid probate?

P robate covers assets that were listed in the sole name of the decedent at the time of his or her death.

Non-probate assets include assets that have a specific beneficiary designation, such as life insurance or employee benefit plans. Non-probate assets also include joint assets owned with rights of survivorship or payable on death type accounts.

Since probate covers assets in the sole name of the decedent, probate can be avoided if the decedent's assets are titled differently prior to his or her death in another fashion, such as in a revocable living trust.

Probate can also be avoided by using joint tenancy with rights of survivorship to title bank accounts or real estate; using payable on death (POD) bank accounts; or using transfer on death securities (TOD).

A qualified estate planning attorney can assist you in properly titling your property to avoid probate and to allow for a smooth transfer to the beneficiaries after your death.

9

What are the advantages and disadvantages of probate?

O ne advantage of going through a probate proceeding is the orderly transition of the estate.

The purpose of a will is not only to ensure assets are distributed according to your wishes; a will also outlines who will oversee the estate assets by serving as executor, what will be required of the executor, the authority of the executor, and who will be appointed guardian of any minor children, among other things.

So, a probate proceeding can be helpful in the straightforward administration of the estate.

Another advantage of probate is, once the executor publishes a notice for unknown creditors, any creditors that do not file claims within the statutory claims period are forever banned from filing claims against the estate.

There are, however, several disadvantages of probate. One is that the estate must stay open for the statutory claims period. As a result, the beneficiaries will not receive their distributions until the claims period has elapsed.

Another disadvantage is the cost of probate, which includes both the time it takes and the fees that are involved.

Finally, when a will goes through probate, your affairs become a matter of public record. Anyone with curiosity may be able to access probate records and glean the financial details of your estate. A living trust is a much more private arrangement allowing for a more discrete handling of your wishes. In only very rare situations do living trusts become public record.

10

I don't have a large estate. Will probate still apply to me?

Yes, unless the size of your estate is under $100,000, you will still have a probate estate. If your total assets are under $100,000, there is currently a simplified method of transfer in Illinois using a Small Estate Affidavit, which takes the place of a formal probate proceeding in court.

If the assets in your name at the time of your passing are over $100,000, however, a probate proceeding is necessary. This is the case whether you have a will or you don't have a will. Of course, having a will is preferable, because you direct in your will who will be in charge and how distributions of your assets will be made, instead of relying upon the statute.

A better route is to have a living trust as part of your estate plan, making sure to title all of your assets in the name of the living trust, so that you avoid having a probate estate altogether. This will ensure that the process that happens after your death will run smoothly, and benefit your family quickly.

11

What is a trust?

A trust is a legal entity created by a trust document that holds the title to assets for the benefit of the maker of the trust (the settlor) or other beneficiaries named by the settlor in the trust. There are many types of trusts that vary according to the needs and desires of the settlor.

A trust allows you to name an individual, an institution, or sometimes both, as co-trustees, to manage the assets you place in the trust. If you die or become incapacitated, the trustee can immediately manage the trust to ensure that you, your spouse, and your dependents are cared for.

Having a living trust can eliminate the need for a guardianship proceeding for you, if you develop a disease that precludes you from acting as the trustee of your trust, such as Alzheimer's or dementia. It can also eliminate the need for a probate estate upon your death, and so it can be a very useful document to include in your estate plan.

12

What is a living trust?

A living trust is one of the most common trusts. It is effective during the settlor's lifetime, and is funded with assets transferred to the trust by the settlor.

A living trust holds the legal title to property. During the lifetime of the grantor (the maker of the trust), the grantor of the trust has full ownership rights in the trust, just the same as the grantor would have owning the property outside of the trust. The trust document dictates how the trust property will be distributed at the death of the grantor, and so it is one of the best ways to avoid probate.

13

What is the difference between a revocable living trust and a testamentary trust?

A living trust is an agreement that is now "alive," as it holds title to assets. The trustee is generally you, while you are alive, and you are holding the title to these assets as the trustee of the trust. The living trust provides for you—while you are alive and upon your death—and provides for your beneficiaries, after having paid your final bills, your taxes, and other obligations.

Since the living trust is "alive" presently and owns assets, one of the biggest advantages of using this trust is that your successor trustee can take over for you when you are no longer able to manage your affairs (this is determined by your physician). That successor trustee can manage your assets, make sure your bills are paid, and pay what is necessary for your care during your lifetime.

A living trust may be amended or revoked at any time during your life, unless you provide otherwise in the trust document. Most people like to be able to revise the trust as life circumstances change. You may also change your trustees, beneficiaries, and any other terms at your discretion.

A testamentary trust is one that is created through a will, and only becomes "alive" after your death and when it receives funds from your estate after your death. It does not provide for you during your lifetime, such as if you have Alzheimer's or dementia and cannot manage your own affairs. A testamentary trust only takes care of your beneficiaries after your death.

14

What is an irrevocable life insurance trust?

M any times people own life insurance policies on their life. Some of these people may have assets that exceed the federal estate tax exemption, which is presently $5.43 million. If these life insurance policies are owned by that person at death, the life insurance will be taxable in the person's estate at a starting rate of about 35% of federal estate tax.

In that situation, a better route is to set up a separate trust, called an Irrevocable Life Insurance Trust, for the benefit of your family. Like its name suggests, the trust cannot be changed by you during your lifetime. At death, the trustee will pay the funds out to your beneficiaries or hold the funds in trust for your beneficiaries, as you have directed in the trust. The significant difference here is that if this is done correctly, the life insurance will not be taxable to your estate at death. For instance, if your estate's tax rate was 40% and you had a life insurance policy in that trust in the amount of $1.0 million, your estate could save approximately $400,000 in federal estate taxes.

This trust will hold life insurance policies on your life. The trustee will pay the premiums for the policies from other assets that you contributed to the trust, or from annual gifts that you are making to the family through the trust.

Since there are serious consequences if this process is done incorrectly—for example, the life insurance proceeds can be held to be taxable to your estate by the IRS—this technique is best done using the services of a qualified estate planning attorney, who has experience in having done these trusts before.

15

What is the benefit of having my trust own my life insurance?

T he benefit of having the irrevocable life insurance trust own the insurance on your life is that the life insurance policy is not an asset of your estate and, if done correctly, will not be taxed for federal estate tax purposes.

This can be significant when one considers that the rate of tax for federal estate tax purposes is 40% on amounts that exceed the federal estate tax exemption.

As irrevocable life insurance trusts have their complexities, it is important to work with a qualified estate planning attorney, who has experience having handled this type of trust.

16

How does an irrevocable life insurance trust work?

After your estate planning attorney has prepared this trust and obtained a federal employer's identification number, the next step is working with a qualified life insurance broker to obtain the right policy for your needs.

The best practice is for the trustee of the irrevocable life insurance trust to apply for the life insurance, which is done that way to keep the insurance policy from being part of your taxable estate. If you are unable to qualify for life insurance yourself, you still may be able to qualify for a second-to-die type policy. If that does not work, but you have life insurance in your own name, you may be able to transfer these policies to the irrevocable life insurance trust. However, in order to keep this insurance from becoming taxable to your estate, you generally need to survive the transfer by three years.

In addition to the life insurance policies, the trust may also own additional assets, such as cash or marketable securities, that you may have transferred into the trust. This will provide funds in the trust to pay the annual premiums. In the event that you do not make such a transfer, then you will be making an annual gift to the trust for the benefit of the beneficiaries of the trust, which they technically have the right to withdraw, and when they do not withdraw it, the trustee can use it to pay the premium. The trustee of the trust has to send notice to the beneficiaries of the trust of their right to withdraw and give a certain time frame for the withdrawal. Normally, each beneficiary will sign a form, known as a "Crummey" notice (based on the name of a court case), which will waive their right to withdraw the gifted amount.

Upon your death, the trustee files a claim to obtain the proceeds of the life insurance policies. Since this type of trust may also be used to provide liquidity to your estate, the trust may have provisions in it that allow the trustee to trade the insurance proceeds to your estate for other, less-than-saleable assets of equivalent value. Alternatively, the trust may allow the trustee to purchase assets from your estate, which will also create liquidity in your estate to pay off your bills and taxes.

Once this is done, the balance of these funds are then deposited with the trustee into the trust account and either paid out or held in trust for the benefit of your beneficiaries, according to your wishes as set forth in the trust.

Since this type of trust has its complexities, it is best to work with a qualified estate planning attorney, who can lead you through the steps that are necessary to properly set up and manage the irrevocable life insurance trust.

17

Can I amend an irrevocable life insurance trust?

Y ou can't change or terminate this type of trust—it is irrevocable!

If that trust owns a life insurance policy, the trustee can cash it out and stop paying the premiums. The amount received from cashing in the insurance cannot be given back to you, but has to be paid to the beneficiaries, according to the terms of this trust.

You need to consider the reasons to use this type of trust and speak with an experienced estate planning attorney before utilizing it.

18

I have a life insurance policy. Can I transfer ownership of it to an irrevocable life insurance trust?

Yes, an existing life insurance policy can be gifted to this trust.

However, there are additional gift tax issues if you do.

For example, you must be alive for at least three years from the date of the transfer, or the policy may be taxable in your estate, because under the tax law, it is considered to be a transfer made in contemplation of death.

19

How do I choose who should be the trustee of my irrevocable life insurance trust?

Another important consideration when you are thinking about this type of trust, or when you are actually setting it up, is selecting a trustee.

The trustee has several important responsibilities, including setting up the trust fund and investment accounts; choosing the insurance company and policy that the trustee will buy on your life; receiving the cash gifts that you make to the trust; notifying trust beneficiaries of these gifts, using the required notices; filing annual federal and state income taxes, which allow the statute of limitations to run on the gift three years after the return was filed; and paying the life insurance premiums each year.

This is a very particular type of trust with specific requirements. If these are not followed precisely, the penalty can be that the life insurance policy will be included in the estate, and you will lose out on the estate tax benefits you sought when making the trust in the first place. Therefore, choose wisely!

20

How do I set up an irrevocable life insurance trust?

Your first step should be to consult a qualified estate planning attorney to help you determine if you need such a trust.

In addition, you also want to add two other members to the team:

- An insurance broker, who can help select the best insurance product for you and can fill in all the necessary paperwork; and

- A Certified Public Accountant (CPA), who can assist in tax planning and tax preparations for the trust returns.

Your estate planning attorney will be drafting the trust, according to your wishes and according to the requirements of the law. Your attorney will be handling the "Crummey" notices, as required to acknowledge the withdrawal rights that the beneficiaries have from the annual gift that you make to the trust to pay the premiums.

Your estate planning attorney will be working with an insurance broker to ensure that the insurance product you select makes sense for you, and to make sure that the application for the new policy is done by the trustee of the trust.

Your estate planning attorney will also be working with your CPA, with respect to the annual gifts that are made. The CPA will handle any gift tax returns that may be required for the gifts that are made on an annual basis.

21

What is a charitable remainder trust?

A charitable remainder trust is a tax-exempt, irrevocable trust.

The most common charitable remainder trusts are annuity trusts and unitrusts. With a charitable remainder trust, you establish a trust and receive income from that trust for a certain number of years, after which time the balance in the trust is transferred to the charity of your choice.

There are several benefits to using a charitable remainder trust. First, you or your beneficiaries will receive income from the trust for a period of years.

Second, you can take a charitable deduction for a portion of the gift in the year the trust is formed. This can help you to avoid the immediate capital gains tax on appreciated property that you would be selling to diversify your portfolio.

Third, using a charitable remainder trust can help reduce or eliminate estate taxes, as the assets are no longer considered to be a part of your estate.

And lastly, a charitable remainder trust allows you to ensure that your gift goes to the charity of your choice upon your death.

22

How does a charitable remainder trust work?

Since this is a highly specialized type of trust, you first need a highly qualified estate planning attorney to set up the trust.

Once it is set up, you can transfer cash and appreciated assets into the trust.

During your lifetime, or during a certain time frame, you can either receive an annuity from this trust, or you can receive a certain percentage of the fair market value of the assets each year.

Then, the charities which you have selected can receive proceeds from the trust as remainder beneficiaries.

23

What are the income tax benefits of a charitable remainder trust?

Many people use a charitable remainder trust when they are ready to sell an asset that is highly appreciated in value. This may include stock that you received as a gift many years ago, or even closely held stock in a family business in which you have an interest.

At the time of the sale of stock, there will be an income tax that will have to be paid by you on the difference between the sales price and your cost basis in the item being sold. The cost basis on shares that you may have received by gift is the original cost basis of the original owner that you received it from. That cost basis is then adjusted for any stock dividends or splits that may have happened over the years. As a result, the gain may be a large gain. Depending on the capital gains tax rate at the time of sale, the income tax that results may also be large.

Another option would be to gift that stock into the charitable remainder trust. The trustee of the charitable remainder trust then sells the stock, with no income tax paid, as it is considered a type of charity. As stated in its name, the remainder of the trust will be paid to public charities that you have selected.

Since the remainder goes to public charities, you may be able to receive an income tax deduction for the value of the remainder interest that is given to charity, taken in the year of the gift. The amount of the deduction that you will be able to take is based upon a number of factors, such as the payout rate that you select for the trust, your life expectancy or the number of years that the trust will be in existence, the fair market value of the gift that you made, the type of property that you gifted, and the Applicable Federal Rate (AFR) published by the IRS monthly.

The determination of this income tax deduction is done in the year of the gift. This income tax deduction may lower your overall income tax in the year of the gift.

24

Can I serve as the trustee of my own charitable remainder trust?

Yes, you can act as your trustee of your own charitable remainder trust.

While many people choose to serve as their own trustee of their charitable remainder trust, many, due to the complexity of the tax issues involved in this area of tax law, turn to a corporate trustee. The federal tax code is very complex in the area of charities, and the method of investing the assets contained in a charitable remainder trust is quite different from that of a normal portfolio.

If you do choose to act as your own trustee, be sure to surround yourself with a qualified estate planning attorney, a qualified Certified Public Accountant, and a great financial advisor who has experience in investing the assets of charitable remainder trusts.

25

If I have a living trust, do I still need a will?

A will is a necessary part of your estate planning. It is a companion document to your living trust.

Once you establish a living trust, you must remember to transfer your assets into the trust. There are times, however, when part of your assets are not in the name of your living trust. For instance, perhaps you inherited property before you died, which did not get transferred into the name of the trust. Or maybe you sold an asset, and the funds are sitting in an account in your sole name while you decide what to do with these funds.

Although your living trust has all of the provisions for the distribution of your assets after your death, the will acts as a funnel for those assets that you did not title into the name of the trust. Many in the legal profession refer to the will as a "pour over" will, as whatever assets that are in your sole name at death will pour over into the living trust, where they will be combined with other assets and be held or paid out according to the terms of the living trust.

It is important to retitle your assets into your living trust during your lifetime, or the assets that are in your sole name may have to pass through a probate proceeding to be "poured over" into the living trust.

 A will is also important because it allows you to appoint a guardian for any minor children that you may have as of your date of death.

There is nothing worse to see in court: relatives fighting about who should be the guardian of your children, especially since the funds that may be held for your children may help to offset the expenses of those who want to be guardian while your children are living with them.

26

If I have a will, will my family still need to do a probate proceeding in court?

A will is really your instruction book. It outlines who will be appointed the executor, what the executor's powers will be, and what each beneficiary will receive.

It does not eliminate a probate proceeding in court, unless your total assets in your estate are under $100,000, where a simplified approach may be used.

Your will also appoints a guardian for your minor children, and states how you want your assets distributed—to your family, your friends, your church, or to another charitable organization.

Having a simple will is better than having no will at all, because you are leaving instructions regarding your estate, but it's still not as good as some other techniques that you can use with your estate, such as combining the will with a living trust.

If your assets are listed solely in your name at your death, it will be necessary to open a probate estate and to appoint an executor, who will liquidate your assets, pay your taxes, pay your remaining bills, and distribute your assets.

There are ways to keep from needing a probate estate, however. The Gierach Law Firm has prepared thousands of estate plans, including wills and trusts, which are designed to preclude the necessity of a probate estate.

27

If I have a living trust, will my family still need to do a probate proceeding in court?

Many times, what people don't understand is which documents (wills or trusts) control over which assets, depending on how those assets are titled.

If you have your assets all titled in your living trust, then the living trust is going to control them, and you won't need to open a probate.

Many times people have a living trust, but they never bother to retitle their assets into the trust name. In that case, if your assets are listed solely in your name, there would be a probate.

Also, if your assets are titled in joint name, neither the will nor the trust controls their disposition, as they go to the surviving joint tenant, by operation of law.

If the assets are titled in your sole name at death, you are guaranteed to need a probate estate, unless your total assets are under $100,000, where there may be simplified procedures available.

A lot depends upon how things are titled – not just the fact that you have the right documents.

Most attorneys who state that they specialize in estate planning, wills, and trusts do nothing to transfer those titles, instead leaving it up to you to initiate and make the transfers.

The attorneys at The Gierach Law Firm, however, work closely with you to ensure all of the transfers are made into the proper trust name, which will avoid the necessity of a probate estate.

28

Why has my attorney not recommended a trust to me?

M any times attorneys don't recommend that you create a living trust because their billing will be larger if your estate goes into probate when you die.

I hate to say it that way, but for some lawyers this is true. At a recent estate planning/ wills and trusts conference, several attorneys present stated that they did not recommend living trusts for just this reason: the potential fee from the inevitable probate estate was higher than the cost of setting up a living trust.

In some jurisdictions, the attorney's fee is a percentage of the value of the estate. In other jurisdictions, where compensation is done on an hourly basis, the attorney's fees earned from probating the estate greatly exceeded the cost of having a well-drafted will and living trust, and transferring your assets into the name of the trust.

Believe it or not, spending the time and money to have an attorney draft your living trust and retitle your property into the trust name is a good thing.

You are, in fact, making an investment for your future. A living trust will protect your interests while you are alive if you are unable to act for yourself, instead of requiring a guardianship estate and, of course, will avoid a probate estate upon your passing.

We at The Gierach Law Firm want everything to be organized for your family, so they don't have to manage difficult issues at a critical point in your life or upon your death. We will work with you to devise the right estate plan for your situation, prepare the appropriate documents, retitle to your assets, give you peace of mind, and ultimately save your estate money.

29

Will my money be tied up if I use a living trust?

Many people think that just having a trust itself ties up their money, and they can't have access to it. Really, nothing can be further from the truth. You have complete control of your finances just like you did before.

When you create a trust, you're making sure that you have a successor trustee, and you are providing instructions for that successor trustee. Those instructions outline your wishes on how to manage those funds, how to take care of you, should it become necessary during your lifetime, and how to handle your wealth on behalf of your beneficiaries when you die.

It is not something that is meant to tie up assets while you are alive.

30

Will the administration of my estate take years?

T he minimum time a probate estate needs to be open in court is for the claims period, which is the time during which claims may be filed by creditors of the deceased. In Illinois, the claims period is six months.

Illinois requires that all taxes be paid and accepted by the federal and state agencies. If a federal estate tax or an Illinois estate tax return are required to be filed, that generally must be filed and accepted by the federal and state government before the estate can be closed.

The federal estate tax return is due nine months after the date of death. The acceptance of that return may be within about six months after that date.

However, if there are any issues that involve valuation questions in the estate, it may take up to a year and a half to settle those issues with the IRS.

As a result, the executor generally does not make a full distribution of the estate until the acceptance letter is issued by the IRS, although they may make a partial distribution prior to that date.

31

If my assets are owned jointly with my spouse, do I still need a will or trust?

T he old style of estate planning was to use joint
tenancy assets. The thinking was that upon the first
to die, the remaining person—the survivor of the two—
would receive all of the proceeds of the account.

That's fine, except that spouses do travel together. If both
of you perished in a common accident, there would be a
probate estate required for the second to die.

If your assets are owned jointly with your spouse, this
does not eliminate probate or the necessity of the process,
it just postpones it until the death of the second to die. It

also does not help you in the event that you or your spouse—or both—are incapacitated due to dementia or another condition during your lifetime.

32

Is life insurance on my life taxable to my beneficiaries upon my death?

T hat question presupposes that there is only one tax to worry about.

From an *income* tax standpoint, life insurance is generally not taxable to your beneficiaries.

There may be some interest that's earned from the date of death until the payment is made, and that interest portion may be taxable.

From an *estate* tax standpoint, the proceeds of life insurance, if you own that policy on your life, are taxable in your estate.

So, for federal estate tax purposes, your life insurance on your life is taxable.

That being said, the size of your estate at the date of your death also affects if it will be taxed.

If your estate is *under* the amount of the exemption that is allowed at that time, your estate will not pay estate taxes on the insurance proceeds.

If, conversely, your estate is *over* the exemption amount allowed, that same life insurance will be subject to estate taxes.

If your estate is larger than the exemption allowed, there is another option to avoid paying taxes on your lifetime insurance proceeds: using a particular kind of insurance trust. You should discuss this option with your estate planning attorney.

33

Are my IRA and 401(k) proceeds taxable to my beneficiaries upon my death?

M ost people forget that IRAs and 401(k)'s are tax deferred vehicles. That means that you are receiving a deduction, or someone else had received a deduction, when the money went into those accounts. No one has paid taxes on the accounts as they've built up and increased in value over time.

When you die, your 401(k)'s and IRA accounts, whatever their values are, are taxable in the federal *estate* tax return. In addition, the beneficiary who receives the money out of the accounts is also taxed on an *income* tax basis for the money they pull out.

Most people do not know that, in addition to the income taxes that will have to be paid on the distribution, the entire account will be subject to estate taxes when you die.

If the fair market value of your estate when you die exceeds the exemption that is in effect at that time, your entire IRA and your entire 401(k) will be subject to the highest marginal rate for estate taxes and your highest marginal rate for income taxes. The combined taxes on these accounts may exceed 70%!

This is why, many times, it's a good idea to try to roll the funds over into an inherited IRA, if that's available, so that the person can further defer any amounts that come out of those funds from an income tax standpoint.

Under current law, it is allowable to roll funds into an inherited IRA. In an inherited IRA, if the deceased person has already begun to take out their required minimum distributions at the age of 70 ½, the beneficiary must continue to take out the same percentage distributions that the deceased person would have had to take out at their age, if they were still alive.

34

Are there taxes on gifts that I make to my children?

Many people think that the person who receives the gift pays income tax on those funds or the asset that was distributed to them, and this is not true. The gift is not taxable for *income* tax purposes.

On the other side of it, many people think if they make a gift to their children, that they get a deduction for that on their income tax return. This is not true either. You don't get an income tax deduction for the gift.

In fact, when you make a gift to your children, there is a combined gift and estate tax that includes all gifts that you make. Your gift will be subject to that tax.

The gift tax law allows you to have an annual exemption amount. Gift taxes or gifts made during your lifetime that are above the amount of the annual exemption get added back into your federal estate tax when you die.

That means that you can take the appreciation on those assets out of your estate, but the amount that you actually gave—the fair market value on the date of gift—has to be included.

So when you make a gift to your children, two things can happen regarding the gift tax law:

- If your gift exceeds the annual exemption amount, you will then use a part of your lifetime exemption for federal estate tax purposes.

- If you have already used your lifetime exemption, then there will be a gift tax you will need to pay on that gift.

That being said, there are a couple of "freebies." For example, you can pay the medical expenses or educational expenses of your children directly, and that will not be considered a gift that is subject to gift tax. An experienced estate planning attorney can provide more information on other "freebies," as well as general information regarding gift taxes.

35

Is there any way to make the administration of my estate easier on my family when I die?

This is a really good question, and a really big concern for many of my clients.

My clients don't want things to be difficult, they want everything to be organized. One way to really accomplish that is to use a living trust.

An experienced estate planner can put together a plan for you that includes, as its centerpiece, a living trust. The living trust will make things so much easier, as long as that estate planner retitles your assets like they should.

If they don't retitle your assets as part of their service, you've got the wrong estate planner, and you should come to us instead for your estate planning needs. The Gierach Law Firm has over 30 years of experience and can put together a whole plan for you.

And the truth is, the more organized your estate and living trust are, the simpler it is on your family that remains behind.

For instance, if you have a living trust set up and all of your assets retitled into that trust name, with the trust listed as beneficiary of your other assets, the trustee that you appointed in your trust can immediately step into their role with a death certificate and a copy of the trust.

Next, the trustee named in the trust becomes the go-to person. They can start liquidating assets, paying your bills, having your taxes prepared and making distributions.

If you have a more complex estate, or the size of your estate is over the federal estate tax exemption, there are additional taxes to pay, tax returns required, and tax issues to resolve. Planning ahead and organizing your estate in advance will make this process go more smoothly and quickly for your family.

36

If all of my assets are in joint name, or I have named beneficiaries, is it possible that I may still need a will and trust?

M any people think that if they have set up joint accounts for each child, or have already named beneficiaries for their accounts or life insurance, that will negate the need for having a will and living trust.

But there are many other things to consider, such as:

- What happens if the person needs the money in their account for their care? Will the child who was named as a joint account holder be cut out of the estate?

- What if a child who has been named a joint account holder predeceases the owner of the account, and that owner did not change the joint account holder to someone else before they died?

- Did the owner of the account intend to cut out that child's children?

- What if the joint account holder is a minor child at the time of the major account holder's death? Who will handle the account until that child attains the age of maturity?

Once again, the answer to these questions is to make the living trust the centerpiece document of your estate plan, and to title all assets in the trust name. In that living trust, you can provide certain amounts or percentages for each of your children. If any do not survive, you can keep the share in trust for the grandchildren.

37

Isn't a trust a rigid document, and will my beneficiaries have a hard time receiving my assets from it?

In reality, trusts can be very flexible documents and can have provisions based on the beneficiaries' age or behavior.

For instance, if you want provisions in the trust to incentivize your children to be better students, you can include provisions in your documents to reward them with an additional distribution if they have "straight A's."

Another example would be if you have a child that has a drug or alcohol problem, or is a big spender, you can give the trustee the discretion to withhold the principal distributions to that child.

You can even set ages at which time distributions can be made. You can give the trustee the discretion to pay out funds from a trust for the child's health, education, support and maintenance, and best interest. Then, once the child attains the age of 25, they can request one-third of their share, the second third to be paid at 30, and the balance at age 35.

This allows your trustee to guide your child down the right path up until that point, just as you would if you were still alive.

There are many other things that can be done to add flexibility to your trust, depending on your family's circumstances and the skill and experience of your attorney.

38

How is my business affected by my death?

T his is a really good question, because many of the people that we counsel in our firm are business owners, and many people forget that their business will impact their estate plan.

Many times, that business owned by you is a major portion of your assets. The income from the business may support the lifestyle of you and your spouse. Your spouse and/or your children may even be involved in that business. You may have a partner in that business, or you may have no one in the business who can take your place if you die or become disabled. You may also have one child involved in the business, but another not involved in the business.

Also, the business is often where the bulk of a business owner's wealth is. If there is no plan to withdraw the money out of the business, how can the business owner provide for their spouse and family?

If you're a business owner, you need to have a succession plan.

One option for this succession plan is to have your business owned by your trust. Your successor trustee could then take over in the event that you're not able to act, you have a health issue that keeps you from acting, or when you die.

That successor trustee needs to act right away, and determine what your succession plan is: if you're going to sell your business, or if you have other people who can still manage it until it can be sold.

This is a topic that I wish more business owners would spend the time with and actually examine, and put together a written plan, because it is important to remember that there are many business planning issues that need to be dealt with that connect with estate planning.

Some other things to consider include:

- To provide for your family after your death, your trustee should be in charge of the business as the owner. You need a written succession plan or, alternatively, an exit strategy.
- If you have not worked that succession plan out yet, at a minimum, you need to leave a list of companies that could potentially buy your company while it is still viable, to provide assets in your estate for your spouse and children.

These are but a few of the issues that need to be addressed. The Gierach Law Firm has counseled thousands of clients on what is the proper strategy for selling their company upon death or passing it to another generation, and we know the tax consequences of each option.

If you're expecting to pass the biggest part of what you own to the next generation, or you want to protect your spouse, your estate plan needs to be drafted in a way that will include considerations for your business.

39

How do I protect myself in the event that I become incapacitated?

There are several good ways to accomplish this.

One is, you should have a financial power of attorney and a healthcare power of attorney.

The financial power of attorney allows the person whom you appoint to stand in your shoes to help out while you are incapacitated.

In addition to having the powers of attorney, you should also make use of a living trust. The living trust will allow your successor trustee to step in at such time that you are not able to act.

At that point, your assets, your income and your expenses will all be taken care of by that successor trustee.

You will have the protection of someone looking out for your interest, without the necessity of a court proceeding.

40

Is having a living trust expensive to create and maintain?

R eally, it's not. A living trust actually helps you avoid extra costs, and is not expensive to maintain.

When you look at the cost of what it saves you in the way of probate, a living trust is actually the better choice. If you don't use a living trust, your estate may need to be probated after you die. You might even have to have a probate proceeding called a guardianship before you die, if you develop Alzheimer's or dementia, and you cannot manage things yourself.

But these probate proceedings may not be necessary if you have a living trust. A living trust coupled with a financial power of attorney may stop that from happening.

The cost of creating a living trust is generally substantially less than the cost of even one probate proceeding. I have even heard attorneys say that they don't like to do living trusts because they make more money when they handle the probate estates!

Everyone knows that there is a cost to having a probate proceeding in court when you die. But the cost of this probate estate may be lessened or even eliminated by the use of a living trust.

Once the living trusts are created, you only need to change the terms of them when there is a change in your life, such as a divorce, the death of beneficiaries or a trustee, or when the law substantially changes.

From a tax perspective, you most likely won't even file a trust income tax return for your trust at any point during your lifetime.

When you have executed your living trust, there is not a lot of cost to maintain that living trust in the future.

41

Who should I appoint to handle my probate estate?

T his is a quandary, and actually one of the more important questions that people have to answer, because that person is responsible for handling all of the assets of your estate.

The executor starts the probate process by filing a petition to probate the will, an affidavit of heirship, and other documents. During the process of the administration, the executor or trustee will need to gather your assets; prepare an inventory of the assets and have certain of the assets appraised; organize your house so that it can be sold, if that is what your documents direct; liquidate the assets; invest for the short term; handle your lifetime income tax returns; file your federal estate tax returns, along with any state death tax returns; pay your bills; do an inventory; and prepare accountings. They may even have to sell your business.

Those are the jobs of the executor or trustee while they are handling the initial phase of the administration.

Since there are so many technical details involved in the process, the executor normally employs an attorney who is a specialist in probate and estate administration to help them through the probate process. The executor is normally entitled to reasonable compensation for his or her services, as well as payment for expenses advanced on behalf of the estate.

Later, if you have trusts set up for your children, the trustee will need to invest the funds, determine when distributions are proper, based upon the terms of the trust, and handle the annual income tax returns for that trust.

As you can tell, most of these jobs are financial in nature, so the person you should be looking to appoint this roles would be somebody with a financial background and some common sense about how to handle these things.

If you don't have that person in your family, consider using a bank as a corporate executor. This is a good option because, if you own a business, the bank may have a department that helps run those businesses until the next generation comes in, or until the business can be sold.

Alternately, consider coupling a corporate trustee consider with one of your relatives, who can be a co-trustee with that trust company.

Obviously, this is one of the most important issues you will face when determining who will be in charge of your estate, so it is a good idea to give it careful thought.

42

Does the administration of a probate estate tie everything up for years?

I t really depends upon the size and nature of the estate you have.

If your estate is probated, it can be an open and closed probate estate within six months. If there are no tax issues, it takes a lot less time to administer, but the estate has to remain open for at least six months in Illinois.

If your estate is taxable—it's above the lifetime exemption that's granted under the federal law—it might take several years to actually fully administer and close the estate, because there are tax clearance letters that the executor and/or trustee will need to obtain from the federal government in order to close the estate.

It could also take longer if any beneficiaries dispute the provisions of the will or trust, and the disputes need to be handled and tried in court.

So it really depends on the circumstances.

43

What are all of the different kinds of taxes that may be due from an estate?

When you die, some of the following taxes will be due:

- A final income tax return will be due for you for the year in which you die.

- After that, if a probate estate is opened, there will be an income tax return for the decedent's estate, if there's income to report that was earned in the tax year after you died.

- If there is a living trust, and if it has income, that trust will also have to file an income tax return.

- In addition, there are also a federal estate tax return and an Illinois estate tax return.

Many times, even if you are under the federal estate tax exemption, there still may be a reason for you to file a federal estate tax return.

So there are a lot of tax issues that can arise at the time that you die, and having an experienced estate planning attorney can help you avoid or lessen these taxes.

44

Will my family be able to get distributions from the estate or from the trust to live on?

T he answer to that question is, "Yes, but it takes longer to get distribution out of a probate estate."

One reason that distributions might be delayed in an estate is, sometimes a will contest may be filed, arguing that you were under duress when you signed the will, or that you did not have the mental capacity necessary to know what you were signing.

Another reason that distributions could be delayed is that the executor needs to determine and pay the federal and Illinois estate taxes first.

On the other hand, a trustee can make those distributions to your family as soon as they take over as successor trustee, which may be a period of days or weeks after your passing. This makes a big difference in keeping the bills for your spouse's normal living expenses paid promptly after you die.

45

If the size of my total estate is under the amount of the federal estate tax exemption, will my executor or trustee still have to file a return?

E ven if the size of your total assets is under the amount of the estate tax exemption, there are a number of reasons to file a federal estate tax return.

- First, under current federal law, the estate will need to obtain a new cost basis for all of the assets in the estate or trust, which is the date of death value. The federal estate tax lists all of these values, so when the assets are sold, there will be ready access to the new cost.

- Second, if your executor or trustee files a federal estate tax return and the IRS does not challenge the fair market values listed in the return after three years, these values will not be able to be challenged by the IRS thereafter. This is particularly useful if your estate has a total value that is just under the amount of federal exemption.

- Third, under current law, if the first spouse to die does not use the entire federal exemption, the unused portion may be used by the surviving spouse. In order claim the unused portion, a federal estate tax return must be filed, with the election to transfer the unused portion of the exemption to the surviving spouse.

46

How can a will be challenged in court?

A will is challenged in a probate court by filing what is referred to as a "will contest."

In order to file the will contest, you need to have grounds to file it, such as having evidence that the deceased did not have the mental capacity to know what they were signing.

To file a contest based on evidence that the deceased had a lack of mental capacity, objective evidence is needed.

Objective evidence could include:

- The testimony of their current doctor or a specialist
- The testimony of witnesses to the document who thought that the deceased might have been too confused to sign
- The testimony of outside third parties that routinely saw the deceased, such as their barber or hairdresser, their banker, their minister and the like, around the time their will was signed.

Alternatively, another reason to contest a will is that the deceased was under physical, emotional or mental duress to sign a document to benefit someone else, such as the person that was causing the duress.

The burden of proving these circumstances is on the person who is contesting the will, which is not necessarily an easy process.

47

Can a gift made by a donor be challenged after their death?

T his is difficult to do, but not impossible.

The reason that it's difficult to do is that you may not have the information to know whether a gift was meant by the deceased. Nobody knows for sure what the deceased wanted, but perhaps the deceased told an outside third party that a gift was intended.

This is the problem. There's a presumption that a gift was meant to be made—that it was desired by the deceased, called donative intent—and it's up to the person challenging that gift to overcome that particular presumption.

In order to have the intent to make the gift, the donor has to have mental capacity at the time the gift was made and cannot be forced or under duress in making the gift.

Similar to the challenge to a will, in order to challenge a gift, the person who is challenging the gift must present evidence that the person making the gift either lacked the mental capacity to make the gift or was under some form of duress at the time that the gift was made.

Depending on whether or not you have information available to you from an outside third party, you may or may not be able to challenge those gifts.

As a general rule, the further away those gifts are in time from the date of death, the harder that challenge will become.

48

My parents put my brother in charge of the estate, and he doesn't want to give any information to the rest of the family, particularly my other brothers and sisters. What can we do about that?

T his does happen—infrequently, but it does happen—and there are a few reasons why it may occur:

- The child put in charge by the parent believes his or her job should not be scrutinized by his or her siblings.
- The sibling is really disorganized and has not kept adequate records.

Other times, though, the sibling has kept whatever funds or assets that were left at the death of the parent for himself or herself.

Sometimes you have to go to court and have the judge either remove the person from acting as executor, if it's grievous enough, or have that person be directed by the court to give an inventory and an accounting, and to make proper distribution of the property that those other siblings should be receiving.

If the information regarding assets produced by the sibling in charge significantly differs from what the other family members think the deceased should have owned, the court will generally require the sibling who was left in charge to explain what happened to the funds.

There is a court process for this type of situation, and you should hire a qualified attorney who can represent your interests.

49

What if a parent leaves a piece of commercial rental property to their children, but the kids can't agree on anything?

Sometimes a parent leaves everything equally to their children, thinking that they are being fair to all.

They didn't anticipate sibling rivalry, but instead are hopeful their children will pull together at the parent's death and work with each other.

Despite the parent's best intentions, conflicts may arise. This may be because of long standing issues between the children or as a result of pressures put on a child, perhaps by a spouse or due to economic circumstances.

In that case, the siblings may decide to buy out the share of the other. They can obtain an appraisal of the property, and offer to purchase the property from the others at fair market value.

If this is not possible due to financial or other considerations, the sibling who wants to liquidate their share can petition the court to sell the entire property and distribute proceeds.

50

Can a parent give nothing to one child and everything to another child?

A parent is not required to give each child the same amount, or to give a child anything at all. The parent could leave everything to charity or to a new spouse.

Occasionally, a parent will leave the estate to certain children and not to others, for various reasons.

For example, perhaps some children are financially successful and others are not. Or, it may be that emotional problems, health issues of the child, or a child's lack of financial success required more support from the parent during the parent's lifetime.

In that case, a parent will leave their share in trust for the child, to preserve the principal for the child's benefit during their lifetime.

Whatever the reason for the difference in the bequests to certain children, sometimes the other children will feel slighted.

However, unless these children have evidence that the parent lacked capacity or signed the will or trust under duress, the courts will generally allow the parent's plan to go forward.

51

What happens if the will or the trust is ambiguous, or if there are provisions that are lacking?

S urprisingly, this does happen on occasion, and there are a few ways it may occur.

It might be that, when the document was drafted, certain provisions were inadvertently omitted. Another possibility is that the language is confusing or able to be interpreted in more than one way. Or perhaps the drafter didn't anticipate that the person was going to own a particular type of asset requiring more explanation.

If it is the case that the document is ambiguous, you will need to file a suit asking for the court to construe that document, and determine what it actually means. In that event, the court will determine what was missing, if anything.

But in order to file the suit, the language of the trust or the will must be determined to be ambiguous by anyone who reads it—meaning there's no way it could be determined what a decedent's intentions were from the document.

These are all things a court would have to determine. Each side would file their own briefs to state their position for the court to review, and then the court ultimately makes a determination.

The court will look at the four corners of the instrument to try to determine the intent of the deceased prior to looking outside of the document. The court will then make a ruling on what the language should have said.

In Illinois, there is a law that allows all of the parties— executor, trustee, and beneficiaries—to agree to what the language means, in lieu of going to court.

The Executor or trustee then would prepare a settlement agreement incorporating the language and its effect on each party, which becomes binding on all parties and their descendants. This is a method to resolve the ambiguity that may be contained in a will or trust without incurring the cost of going to court to make that determination.

52

How do I find a good attorney to represent me in a probate or trust dispute?

The answer to that is experience. How many years has the attorney practiced in the probate and trust area? How many estate disputes have they represented? How many cases similar to yours have they handled?

These are all great questions to ask when you are searching for an attorney. After all, wouldn't you rather have someone who has experience handling disputes tell you if you have a case or not, and whether you can possibly win it before you start the process?

Probate and trust disputes are a specialized area. Handling such cases requires a skill set different from what an attorney who does personal injury work would have. This skill set is gained from both knowledge and experience.

Although a lawyer may have had training or coursework that taught them the mechanics of these types of disputes, there is no replacement for a lawyer who has experience handling estate or trust disputes. Experience will allow a lawyer to tell you whether you have a good case, how the courts have handled the issues in the past, and what evidence you need in order to win the case.

Another thing to consider when searching for an attorney is to examine your relationship with that attorney. I think the most important thing is to have a good rapport with your attorney. Your attorney has to keep you involved, and make you part of the process.

At Gierach Law Firm, we believe we are that type of attorney and are able to serve you well in this area of the law.

Part II:

Selected Articles by Denice A. Gierach

Denice has written numerous newspaper columns in the Business Ledger, catering to closely held businesses in the Chicago market. In 2008, The Business Ledger named her as one of twenty "Influential Women in Business."

She is also a past monthly contributor to "Dollars and Sense" in the *Naperville Sun,* and in the past, wrote and published her own newsletter. She continues to write blog posts on various subjects that impact her clients.

Selected past articles of relevance have been included here, with slight amendments and additions, when necessary, for the sake of clarity and grammatical correctness.

1

Is this a good time to transfer your wealth to your children?

As published in The Business Ledger, 2009

With the interest rates at a really low rate, and with the economic fallout from the present economy, even people with money do not feel flush now and may decide that they do not want to make gifts to the next generation. Even though the economy has been in recession many times before and has come out of it to prosperity, sometimes it is hard to look beyond the present time to see that prosperity.

However, this is really a good time to consider making gifts. In a low interest rate environment, there are many tools allowed by the Internal Revenue Code, which allow a person to give more than they would in a higher interest rate environment. These tools are given various names by estate planners such as SCINs, GRATs, CLAT's and IDGT's. Since the value of the gift is based upon interest rate tables shown by the IRS, referred to as the "applicable federal rates," and those rates are low, the low interest rates enable you to transfer more of your wealth tax free.

If you think that your children will need to borrow money, and they are a good credit risk, consider acting as their banker. While you must have a note and proper collateral, just like the bank, using the IRS tables published in October of 2008, you can make a nine year fixed rate loan to your child for a rate as low as 2.63%, which your child will not be able to match in the open market. Then you can collect the interest on the note for at least one year and forgive up to $13,000 ($26,000 if your child is married) of your child's obligation each year, without incurring current gift taxes and also decreasing your potential future estate tax liability. The IRS tables for interest change every month, so you will have to consult your tax professional to determine the current rates.

There are other more complex techniques where the low interest rates also help to minimize your future federal estate taxes and are most helpful to those persons with a higher amount of wealth. One concept mentioned above is a SCIN, which is a self-cancelling note. Using this technique, you sell an asset to a family member. You, as the seller, agree to finance the sale and you provide the buyer with a note payable to you which stipulates that the unpaid balance will be cancelled when you die.

Another technique, the GRAT, is called a grantor retained annuity trust, and it allows you to transfer future appreciation on assets that you think may appreciate in the future to your children or other heirs. Assuming that you live longer than the term of the trust, which may be two or three years, the balance in the trust will go to your heirs tax free of either gift or estate tax. However, if you fail to survive the term of the trust, the amount reverts to your estate and may be taxable upon your death.

There is another technique referred to as a CLAT, a charitable lead annuity trust, which is a longer term strategy than a GRAT. While a GRAT will revert to your estate if you fail to survive its term, a CLAT will not. In a CLAT, property is placed in trust for a period of years during which a fixed amount is paid to a charity each year, with the remainder of the trust at the end of the term passing to non-charitable beneficiaries. Using the CLAT, you may receive a large charitable deduction in the first year the trust is set up for the gift portion to the charity, but in that event, you are taxable from an income tax standpoint on the income that is being paid to the charity.

A technique that moves the assets out of your estate immediately and is not dependent upon your survival is a sale to an IDGT, an intentionally defective grantor trust. This trust is perfectly legal and is not actually defective. Using this estate freeze technique fixes the value of the asset that will be includible in your estate.

As you may be able to tell from this article, there are a number of perfectly legal techniques in which you are able to give more to your heirs due to the low interest rate. Since these are more complex techniques, it is wise to use a trust attorney who specializes in this area to assist you in making these types of gifts.◆

2

Consider a Donor Advised Fund

As published in The Gierach Law Firm Newsletter,
September, 2009

M any people give small amounts to numerous
charities, without considering whether and how
to give more of their total charitable gifts to those
organizations that assist in dealing with issues near and
dear to their heart, which may range from scholarships to
educational institutions, research on cancer, Alzheimer's
disease, mentoring programs, helping children, humane
societies, to name but a few. Those larger gifts allow
them to either support an existing program or to create a
program that creates a legacy for their family while

supporting those causes that really mean something to them.

There are a number of ways to support a charity with larger gifts. Some of them are as easy as writing a check or by gifting shares of stock in which the donor has a low cost basis. Another way is using a charitable remainder trust where the donor receives a percentage of the fair market value of the donated assets for his or her lifetime or a term of years, leaving the remainder interest to charity. A method used by Jackie Kennedy Onassis is a charitable lead trust, where a trust is established and the income of the trust is given to the charity and upon the donor's death or after a term of years, the donor's family gets the remainder of the trust.

One of the reasons that donors like a donor advised fund is that they want to train their children on the importance of charitable giving.

Sometimes, a donor wants to provide a gift over time, but also wants to stay involved in the recommendation of a gift to charities of their choice. Such a donor would be using a donor advised fund. Using this type of vehicle does not tie the donor to a specific charity or charitable purpose, as long as the donor does not impose a material restriction or condition on his or her gift. The donated property must be held either by a large public charity or held by a community foundation, such as The DuPage Community Foundation, or there are several brokerage houses who have this vehicle set up to avoid having to handle all of the paperwork and to act as the administrator of the fund.

One of the reasons that donors like a donor advised fund is that they want to train their children on the importance of charitable giving. These funds promote long term commitments supporting very worthwhile causes that the family has supported in the past. This is because the donor and their families or persons designated by them are actively involved in recommending when, how much and to what charities their funds' assets will be distributed.

In comparison to private foundations, donor advised funds are easier and less expensive to create and are subject to fewer restrictions and regulations. Donors can start smaller—the initial contribution may be as small as $10,000 and the donors can build their funds along the way, allowing the grants out of the fund to grow to make a larger gift to finance particular projects such as financing a new piece of medical equipment for a hospital, providing for major grants from the fund in the event of a disaster and the like.

Besides the tax deductions that may be allowed for the use of a donor advised fund, the donor has trained his family on the importance of giving, thereby creating a legacy for the donor's family in the community.◆

3

Giving Back to the Community

As published in Law Talk, The Business Ledger, August 2009

B usiness people generally get a bad rap in the general press and the movies trying to make the business of making money a bad thing. The reality is that many businesses that are successful have a genuine desire to give back to the community, which they do in many ways.

There are literally thousands of charities in the Chicago metropolitan area, all of which need help in the form of donations, manpower or active participation. Charities rely principally on volunteers who provide the service directly to that charity's intended beneficiaries. However, many of them also need business people who can sit on the charity's board and help to direct the business of the charity. Whether your background is in general management, accounting, legal or sales, these charities can use your help in guiding them towards fulfilling their mission of helping people.

Many times it is essential for the business owner board of director to give input to the charity, as the leaders of the charity have no real business background.

If you serve on the board of directors, besides helping to guide the business of the charity, you will also be expected to help raise funds to keep the charity in operation. Many boards expect that you will either "give or get" a certain amount of money to contribute to the charity. This may be contributed to various fundraisers for the charity that you will attend and invite your friends and business contacts.

The need has grown so much in DuPage County, for instance, that many of the charities have outgrown their space and are looking to either lease another space or to buy or build another building. As in any business, there are a myriad of questions that need to be addressed in determining whether to move. Beside the basic one of need, there are many questions as to whether the charity can afford to pay the additional rent or raise the additional capital to build a building, if the new property is in a good location to be accessible to the charity's constituents, if the building has any possibility for growth of the charity in the future, if the configuration of the building will work for the charity, to name but a few. Many times it is essential for the business owner board of director to give input to the charity, as the leaders of the charity have no real business background. They have to rely upon the board to give the proper direction.

If you do not have the time to devote towards being on the board, it is still a good idea for the business owner to participate in their favorite charity by sponsoring various events and providing manpower to help at the different events, which may range from golf outings to galas to ribfests to house raffles to Soup's On, which benefits local food pantries. The types of fundraisers are endless depending on the type of charity.

In addition to the normal fundraisers, there are also many ways to leave your legacy behind and benefit your favorite charity either while you are alive or after you have passed away, using techniques such as the donation of a life insurance policy that you continue to pay the premiums, using a gift annuity, setting up a charitable remainder trust or using a charitable lead trust. Your estate planning attorney should be able to assist you in creating that legacy so that when you are gone, you will be remembered for all the good that you do. Sometimes this memory is in the form of your name on a building or your name on a particular office or laboratory, or a scholarship fund. While this may seem egotistical at first blush, telling your story and your connection to the charity may be inspirational to others who become connected to that charity, and especially to your children, who will find out from you first hand that it is not "always about them."

While all of this is done in the spirit of giving back to the community, you will find that you get many things back from the charity, as well. Besides having fun at the events, you will find that some of the skills that you do not normally use in your business, as that skill has been delegated to another person in your organization, are now useful. You may also find that some of the people on the board become your best friends, based upon this one shared interest in helping out the charity. It is certainly true that in giving back you receive.◆

4

If You Plan to Contest the Will, It is Best to Refuse the Bequest

As published in The Gierach Law Firm Newsletter, September 2009

If a relative of yours dies and leaves you something in their will, but you think that person did not have the legal capacity to make a will in the first place—you do not think that the deceased knew who their family and friends were, what he or she had in general in assets, and that he or she knew that the document that was being signed was their will—then don't accept the bequest in that will, if you are planning to contest it. If that will was declared by the court as not being valid, you might be included in another will at a larger share or you may be the sole heir of the deceased who has no prior will. Perhaps the deceased told you that he or she was leaving a larger share to you. For any of these reasons, you may determine that you will contest the will.

Of course, we are not promoting that people contest their relative's wills, but there are times where a caretaker may be listed in the last will of the deceased, at a time when the relative knows that the deceased did not know who they were, what year it was, or where they were. In that circumstance, it may be appropriate to file a will contest.

If you decide that you wish to file a will contest, it is important that you not accept a bequest made in the will that you are contesting. If you decide to accept such bequest and then fight for your additional share, the court may determine that you elected to take the bequest under the will and your case will be dismissed. This is known in legal parlance as the doctrine of "election," in which the beneficiary cannot simultaneously accept benefits conferred by a will while setting up claims contrary to the document itself. For instance, a decedent left her estate to her surviving child and left only a nominal amount to the children of another deceased child. Those grandchildren accepted their bequest and then filed suit to challenge the validity of the will. The will contest was dismissed, due to the election of the grandchildren in accepting the gift.

In another case, the will provided that the surviving spouse of the decedent had the right to stay in the family residence as long as she wished. As she had a prenuptial agreement, this was her only benefit. She filed a will contest, alleging that her husband did not have the legal capacity to make the will and that the prenuptial agreement was not valid due to the lack of disclosure. The surviving spouse stayed in the residence during the pendency of the will contest. As a result, the court dismissed her lawsuit, stating that she elected to take the benefits under the will.

The amount of the bequest, even if it is personal property, is not relevant. If you accept the bequest, you have elected to take under the will and will be precluded from maintaining your will contest lawsuit, even though a prior will provided you with a significant legacy. Although no Illinois courts have applied this doctrine to trusts, there is every indication that the courts would do so.

The bottom line is if you intend to file a will contest, refuse the bequest.◆

5

Using a Trust to Provide for Long Term Care

As published in The Gierach Law Firm Newsletter, June 2010

As long term health care continues to spiral upwards, it is a good idea to have long term care insurance, which will provide something for both nursing home care and at home care. Beyond long term care insurance, which has its limits, an elder person can plan for long term care while protecting their assets. They do this by using a particular trust known as a Medicaid Trust.

The Medicaid Trust is particular type of trust which allows an elder person to obtain Medicaid assistance to cover the costs of long term care, without using up their own personal assets. In this trust, the individual who creates the trust retains the right to income for life. For most elders, this right to income is the only way they can maintain their standard of living. If the trust is created at least 60 months before the elder person applies for Medicaid benefits, the existence of the trust will not preclude the elder from qualifying for Medicaid benefits to pay for the cost of nursing home care. In addition, the entire principal of the trust may then be protected from the cost of long term care.

For most elders, this right to income is the only way they can maintain their standard of living

There are several issues that an elder needs to be aware of when using this type of trust. First, the elder does not have control of the principal of the trust. While the elder can still control the ultimate beneficiary of the trust when the elder dies, the elder does not control the payment of principal out of the trust from the date of the trust's creation. These trusts are set up with another trustee involved who will determine how much principal will be paid to or for the benefit of the elder person. If the elder retained control and could pay out principal to or for his or her benefit, the elder may be deemed to be in control of the assets despite the trust and the elder may be denied coverage under Medicaid. This lack of control by the elder may be a problem for many elders, although their children may like it since there may be more assets available for them at the death of the elder person.

Another issue is that as more and more baby boomers need assistance to pay for the cost of nursing home care and apply for Medicaid benefits, there may be less money to go around. As a result, the funds in the trust may have to be used for the care of the elder person, which may result in less to be inherited by the elder's family.

In addition, the Medicaid law may also change to have a longer look back provision than 60 months, as a result of the financial pressures of more and more baby boomers applying for Medicaid.

All in all, if the elder person plans ahead and is not bothered by the lack of control or the uncertainty of the law, the Medicaid trust can have advantages for that person. As this is a specialty type of trust, the elder person should consider hiring an expert in this area to help to draw this trust for them.◆

6

Planning for Long Term Care for Aging Parents

As published in The Beacon News, July 2011

I n a community such as Aurora, where there are 23,635 people between the ages of 35-44 (according to the 2000 U.S. Census) many residents may have aging parents and are thinking about what their mother and father's future care may require. As our parents age, it sometimes becomes apparent that the parents are unable to live alone in their own home. The first option may be to provide adequate support for their needs while they live in their own home. This is generally a good option, as the parents are able to stay in their own home. It is a particularly good option if your parents have obtained long term care insurance.

To find out how much various types of long term care should cost, there are several websites, which can help you to compare costs for various types of care for your particular area. For instance, Genworth Financial, one of the country's largest long term care insurance providers, shows local costs at Genworth.com/costofcare. Another big insurance carrier, MetLife, provides area specific information at MatureMarketInstitute.com. Other resources include a Medicare manual called "Medicare and Home Health Care", which describes what home-health care benefits Medicare covers (see Medicare.gov). There is also information at United Hospital Fund's "Next Step in Care" website for family caregivers (nextstepincare.org).

Besides the fact that your parents would generally be happier staying in their own home, the cost of in home services is roughly the same this year as last, according to the Genworth annual survey. However, the charges at assisted living facilities or nursing homes have increased significantly over the same period. For instance, the national median rate for a shared nursing home room climbed by 5.7 percent to $193 per day from 2010 to

2011. The cost of a private room was $213 a day, or a 5.1 percent increase from 2010.

While you may not wish to haggle about the price at a time when your parents need the extra care, if the long term care expense is way above the market rate, it may give you some negotiating strength. Having the knowledge that these websites may provide may allow you to save some real money over time, which is important when you are trying to stretch your parents' money for as long as you can.◆

In 2014, the national median daily rate for a shared nursing home room was $212, an increase of 2.62 percent from 2013. The cost of a private room was $240 a day, an increase of 4.45 percent from the previous year.

7

Talking with Your Elderly Parents about Lifestyle and Money

As published in The Gierach Law Firm Newsletter in two pats, August 2011

T here comes a time in your life when your parents are older and you are watching over them like they may have done for you when you were younger. You worry about them taking their medicines, about eating right, about falls in their home, and about whether they can live on their own any more without assistance. You may also be concerned about whether they are paying their bills or handling their health insurance claims. Another concern is if they can still drive and be safe.

While this is a normal part of the "sandwich generation" where you are looking out for your children and also for your older parents, it is still a difficult time in your life. Of course, your parents wish to keep their independence for as long as possible, just like your children are trying to become more independent from you. Both parents and your children, while appreciating your concern, may resent your intrusion. This article will focus on your parents' feelings about and responses to your concerns.

Making the determination of whether your parents can live on their own depends on their own general health and whether they have their mental abilities still about them. Have they been exhibiting an ability to cook for themselves, clean up after themselves? Are their clothes clean? Is there food in the house for them to eat? Is their mail taken in on a regular basis? Is their bathroom clean? Are they able to get to the store on a regular basis? Are they able to remember to take the medicines prescribed by their physician? If the answer to all of these questions is yes, then your parents may be able to stay on their own for a while.

However, if you notice a deficiency in any of those areas, it is possible that you parents can still live on their own in their own home, but they may need some assistance, ranging from someone who can clean their home or take them to the store, to someone who is on site every day for a certain number of hours a day or having a 24/7 live in assistant. Many times parents may be resistant to this help, which is not deemed to be a positive step for them. While you are looking at it as it helps your parents out and they can continue to live in their own home (both positive steps), your parents may look at it as a loss of their independence and privacy. They might have to acknowledge that they are "slipping," which is a scary concept to them.

There are people who have a specialty in geriatric psychology who can visit with you and your parents so that a joint plan that is agreeable to all the parties can be devised.

If your parents are unwilling to talk with you about it or become agitated with you, one option in dealing with these issues is to hire a person, a geriatric specialist, who can evaluate their situation and make the determination of just how much assistance is needed so that your parents can stay as independent as possible. There are people who may be trained as geriatric nurses, who have a specialty in geriatric psychology, who can visit with you and your parents so that a joint plan that is agreeable to all the parties can be devised. These same people have contacts to help you locate that perfect person to help out—one that your parents will like.

Sometimes, you need help to have those conversations with your parents, when your roles have been reversed. It can give all the parties a better point of view, and give you piece of mind.

> *To ask about assets, liabilities, much less income and expenses, is not deemed to be "polite conversation."*

As you can see, there are many considerations regarding the physical needs that your aging parents may have, and how to deal with those things that your parents are no longer able to do physically, due either from physical infirmity or from a dementia or Alzheimer's condition. But you may also have to talk with your parents about money.

While everyone has been raised a little differently, most of the prior generation has tended to keep their finances very private. Parents, in most cases, have never spoken with their children about what their assets and liabilities are, much less what their income and expenses are. To ask about these things is not deemed to be "polite conversation". Yet, as our parents age, how do you know whether your parents are paying their bills or even have enough money to pay their bills? If they needed extra care, could they afford it? Is their home paid for?

Handling your own finances is one of the badges of independence that you possess. It is difficult to have those discussions with your parents about their finances, but there are several suggestions that may be helpful.

One suggestion may be that you have recently worked with a financial planner on your own finances and were very pleased. You may suggest that your parents do the same and maybe use the same person for their financial planning.

Another suggestion might be that you have also done your estate planning, perhaps using a living trust as part of your estate planning. You may suggest that your parents should consider doing that as well, which would protect the surviving spouse and make sure that their bills are paid during times of infirmity. As part of the estate planning process, your parents will need to name successor trustees to themselves, which will probably be you. That will at least ensure that you will be able to take over for them in the event that they are no longer able to act. Most trusts have language whereby their children and your parents' physician determine when they no longer have the mental capacity to act as trustee.

Sometimes, with a living trust in place, a recalcitrant parent may find it acceptable to allow you to be a co-trustee with that parent while they are alive. This may allow you to gain access to their financial records to make sure their bills are paid, that checks have been deposited and their financial investments properly monitored. Sometimes that parent is gradually just losing interest in taking care of paying the bills. Perhaps, you can offer to write out the checks for the bills for their signature, as a first step in having the parent accept your assistance.

There is no magic formula for breaking the ice on this subject. There is also no magic age that turning over management of financial assets should take place. We have all seen cases of parents in their 90's still being sharp and perfectly capable of taking care of their own finances. We have also seen cases where the parent is in their 70's and is not capable of doing so, due to physical or mental infirmity.

You will know when it is time. Using your own case as an example of you doing financial planning or estate planning may open the door to conversations with your parents that may result in their financial futures being properly managed and having an adequate plan for the future.◆

8

Use of Powers of Attorney for Your Children Who are Over 18

As published in The Gierach Law Firm Newsletter, February 2007

W hen your children go to college, they are generally at least 18 years of age. In Illinois, they are considered to be adults at that time. This means that you, as their parents, are not legally entitled to their school information, which includes grades—despite the fact that you are footing the bill for the tuition. It also means that if there is a medical issue or if your child has a psychological or emotional issue, you are not entitled to know what it is. The hospital, doctors, nurses, school psychologists, etc. will not talk with you to tell you what the problem is, unless your child specifically authorizes you to do so at that time. At the time that you are needed, your child may not wish to tell you about the situation, in the case of a psychological issue, an emotional issue or a drug issue. In the case of a physical infirmity, your child may not be able to tell you about it. In any event, that leaves you, as the parent, unable to give proper assistance to or for the benefit of that child.

The hospital, doctors, nurses, and school psychologists will not talk with you to tell you what the problem is with your child

One way to deal with this is to have your child sign a financial Power of Attorney, naming you as their agent to deal with financial matters for them or health care matters, as well. With this document, you should be able to receive their full tuition and room and board bills, reconcile their bank accounts, if needed, receive their grades to see that your money is going for good use, and most importantly, to get medical information about them, especially in the event of an accident or other medical need. It is important that the Power of Attorney contain the necessary HIPAA authorization language in the document so that you will be able to access their medical information.

There are times that the child does not feel comfortable naming you, the parent, as their agent. They are just beginning to live on their own and feel that their independence is threatened. In that event, it is important that they name someone, perhaps an older sibling or another family member, to be there to offer assistance when needed.

Using a Power of Attorney for your child over 18, who is legally an adult, is one of those things that you don't think about until the need arises, and then it is too late to obtain the document that would protect your child. Don't wait until it is too late! ◆

9

Are You an Innocent Spouse?

As published in The Gierach Law Firm Newsletter, June 2011

A re you considered an innocent spouse for tax purposes? What is an innocent spouse and is there a protection for innocent spouses?

Most couples file joint income tax returns as a married couple. This means, generally, that both parties are responsible for what is on the return, as well as what income should be reflected on the return, but is not.

Sometimes the division of labor between husband and wife is such that one of the parties handles the tax return. Sometimes that person places the returns in front of the non-preparing spouse and that spouse signs the returns, not knowing or checking the information in the returns for accuracy. Worse still are cases where the preparing spouse signs both names to the returns and the non-preparing spouse has no clue that the return was ever prepared, filed or what was in the return.

As a result, if the preparing spouse prepares the returns and substantially underreports the income earned, both parties are responsible for the additional tax, interest and penalties that ensue because of the action of the one spouse. Sometimes the unreported income is a result of fraud, gambling, drugs or other illicit activities. The non-preparing spouse may claim that he or she did not have any knowledge of the underreporting—and they may genuinely not have any knowledge—but still may be held responsible by the IRS.

There is a procedure to request "innocent spouse" relief from the IRS, which involves filing an IRS Form 8857, which needs to be filed within two years from the date that the IRS files a levy notice for the tax owed. A person who needs to use this form and request this relief should go to a qualified professional, as certain documents should be attached to the form. The IRS has denied about 2,000 of the 50,000 taxpayers that apply for relief each year, just for filing for this relief after the two year period has elapsed.

It is important, if the usual non-preparing spouse suspects their partner of failing to include income or of making up expenses, that non-preparing spouse file a separate return. That way that spouse will not be liable for the tax mess created by the other spouse.

Another thing that people may not know is that the IRS can legally disregard a divorce decree. Even if that decree holds you harmless or states that the other party is responsible for the IRS problems, the IRS does not have to follow that provision. That just means that if the IRS comes after you for the entire amount and your former spouse has any assets, you may go after him or her to recover the amount pursuant to that section of the decree. At that point, though, that former spouse probably has no assets to recover or even to pay the IRS their due.

Sometimes an abusive relationship keeps one spouse from taking action or filing a separate return. If this happens, it is recommended that spouse keep a diary or other record to support their fears, which may come in handy later.

Although the IRS will allow the innocent spouse rule to protect some spouses, it is always a better route not to have to trust that they will. If in doubt, file a separate return.◆

10

Is Your House in Order?

As published in The Beacon News, April 2011

I read an interesting question recently, which brought back to me why we do estate planning at our firm. The question was:

"If something happens to you today, how would your family be affected tomorrow?"

Estate planning focuses on wills and trusts, powers of attorney and the potential for guardianship. The documents that are completed during estate planning are meant to protect your family in the event that something happens to you. This may be that you have died in an accident, or you may be still alive, but unable to care for yourself. While we cannot predict the future, without you having these documents in place, the only certainty is that your family will be relying on the statute and what that statute says that your family will have to do.

The documents that are completed during estate planning are meant to protect your family in the event that something happens to you.

For instance, if you are alive, but unable to care for yourself, your family will have to go to court to have you declared incompetent to manage your own affairs and have a guardian appointed. The guardian may be someone that you might desire or it may be another person that you would not have selected. The court might have preferred a spouse to be the guardian, who might be overwhelmed at your condition and dealing with the physical nature of it.

A better approach would be to have your road map set out in the estate planning documents that you complete. Instead of a guardian, you may have a financial power of attorney that you have appointed in a document who starts in that position at such time as you become disabled, coupled with a living trust that selects a trustee to act if you are unable to do so. That trustee will pay your bills, invest your assets, make sure that your income is deposited and in general, do whatever you may currently do for yourself.

So, if you are still not convinced to do your estate planning, as it is not enough for you to wonder how your family will cope with the financial aspects of your disability or death, what if you also have either minor children or you have children or family members with special needs? Who will be their guardian and care for them? A child in Illinois is considered to be an adult at the age of 18. Is that the age that you want that child (now considered an adult) to obtain your wealth? Imagine that you have two minor children, an estate of $2.0 million and no spouse that survives you, do you want your children to each receive the amount of $1.0 million at age 18?

The situation is more pronounced if you have a child born with special needs. Who will care for that child in the event that you are not around to do so? In addition to having a provision in your will to appoint a guardian, you will also need to file guardianship proceeding in court at about the time that child will attain the age of 18, as that child is considered an adult at age 18, in spite of any medical condition to the contrary. This means that you are not able to even inquire about medical issues, as the HIPPA law does not allow you to do so.

The purpose of this article is not to scare you or make estate planning more complex than it is, but rather to suggest that you should be more proactive in these uncertain times. While many times, clients are uncertain about what choices to make, the worst choice is the one that is not made. Most documents are not irrevocable and you can change the choice if you later determine that you need to. Not making a choice is making a choice.◆

11

Taking Care of Mom and Dad when They are Elderly

As published in The Business Ledger, 2009

Most clients talk with their attorneys about what may happen to them as they become older and are unable to care for themselves. Most express a definite desire to not have to stay in a nursing home, as they view such places to be very depressing and they want to stay in their own homes. However, if such clients are unable to care for their own needs, they may not be able to stay in their own homes without proper assistance. This may require the hiring of an experienced caretaker, which may not only be costly, but sometimes is not a good fit for such elders.

Sometimes the children of such elders are willing to care for their parents, even if it means that such child foregoes their employment, as many times this is a full-time care position. This is true even if the children are not qualified nursing staff. Some children are willing to take care of their elderly parents without receiving any compensation for doing so, and perhaps such children do not need the income to live on.

Many times the parents acknowledge that this care may be needed in the future and also that they would feel comfortable having one of their

Caregiver agreements provide terms about the cost and quality of the care that will be delivered to the elderly parent.

children care for them in the comfort of their own homes. The parents understand the tremendous sacrifice of time this may be for the child and so may wish to do a caregiver agreement. This is a formal contract in which a child or other relative is hired to care for elderly family members. The payments under these agreements are not considered gifts, which is an important consideration if the elderly person later wishes to apply for Medicaid or other governmental assistance programs, to provide for nursing home care at some point. Instead, the payments under these agreements are considered compensation to the recipient, subject to income taxes.

These agreements provide terms about the cost and quality of the care that will be delivered to the elderly parent. The contracts should specify the duties that are expected to be performed, i.e. making sure that medications are given, preparing and serving meals, running errands, keeping the parent's house clean and tidy, paying bills, etc. The compensation is based upon the average hourly rate that local agencies would charge for the service, which may be $12 to $20 per hour for personal care services to substantially more for geriatric care management services. The agreement should stipulate how the payment will be made, such as payments in regular installments like a paycheck. Since the compensation is taxable to the child giving the service, the contract will have to cover whether the child is considered an independent contractor, in which they have to pay the payroll taxes on the money that they receive, or an employee, where the parent would have to hire a payroll service to manage the payments of payroll taxes.

If neither the parents nor children did a caregiver agreement, but the parent needs care and the child is willing to provide it, is there a way to get compensated for such assistance? The Illinois statute allows a relative of a disabled person who takes care of the disabled person by personally living with and taking personal care of the disabled person for at least three years to file a claim against the disabled person's estate after he or she dies. This claim takes into account the caretaker's lost employment opportunities, lost lifestyle opportunities and emotional distress experienced as a result of personally caring for the disabled person. The claim also may be reduced by any financial advantage that the caretaker may have received while caring for the disabled person and the factors are listed in the statute. Depending on the person's disability and the assets available, the potential compensation may be up to $180,000, if the disabled person is 100% disabled.

It is still a good idea for parents to plan ahead to make sure that as they age, they will be cared for in a manner that they choose. If they don't choose, the choice will be made for them.◆

12

So You Are Retired—Now What?

As published in Law Talk, The Business Ledger, September 2009

N ow that you have made the decision to retire (or the decision was made for you by the company that you worked for as a result of the economy), it is time to decide what to do with your life. While you may want to take some well-deserved time off, try to set out a timeline for that "vacation" and a self-imposed deadline to make the decisions for your future. Remember that your prior job did not define you and may be just the stepping stone to something that you always wanted to do in your life, but were unable to do as a result of your obligations or other circumstances.

Even the most avid golfers may decide that they need something more to do than golf.

Many people may think that golf is "it", but even the most avid golfers may decide that they need something more to do than golf. If you are very active in your community in various charitable organizations, you may quickly fill your time in a very satisfying way. If you are not that active, consider the old adage—"For better, for worse, but not for lunch." Your spouse, who may already be retired or not working, will be happy to help you make decisions that will be right for you to keep you active.

One thing that you may find satisfying is to become a consultant. Many people who retire or are severed by their former employer continue their relationship with their former employer by becoming a consultant to that employer. Your former employer probably severed the relationship in order to save costs and survive in this economy, understanding that your employer saves not only your gross wages, but also 30 – 40% in benefits. That company does need to have the expertise that you provided filled in another way. Either the company hires someone at a much lesser rate than you with a lot less experience or they hire a consultant to do the same job.

From your point of view, you can choose to work what hours you want, using your expertise and what you already know about the business and the issues that are involved. You will receive compensation that will generally be a fair rate, based upon the number of hours worked. You will have to pay taxes on that income yourself—income taxes, social security taxes and Medicare taxes—all of which were previously done by your former employer.

Many times the company that you will be consulting for will require that you form an entity such as a limited liability company or a corporation, so that entity will be the consultant with your former employer. This entity will protect your other assets from potential liability and also protect your former employer from any claim that you are still an employee, thereby cutting off any potential rights to the 30-40% benefits that the former company would be responsible for in the event that you were still an employee.

Once you have that entity created, if you find that you enjoy being a consultant, you can sell your entity's services to other companies, as well. You know the industry that you were in and may find that you will enjoy serving other companies, as well as your prior employer. That being said, you need to make sure that you have not signed any previous noncompete agreements with your former employer, the language of which will preclude you from selling your talents to companies that compete with your former employer. Even with those restrictions in place, it is a good idea to remain active in a trade association for the industry that your former company was in, as the restrictions will not last forever and you may find that there are other companies that are active in the trade association that may need your services.

You may be eligible to set up your own benefit packages for your new business that may be advantageous to you, both economically and from a tax perspective. You should consult your attorney and your accountant to determine what entity is right for you and what benefits you may be eligible to have in your business. These may range from healthcare reimbursement plans or normal health insurance to 40l(k) plans. All of this will require some tax planning on your part with your attorney and accountant.

For those of you who think that life has just ended because you have lost your job—think again. The best part of life may still be ahead—now you can build the job of your dreams. ◆

13

Are you Organized if Something Happens to You?

As published in The Naperville Sun, July 2008

If you become disabled suddenly through a car accident or health calamity, will your family or significant other know what your wishes are? If you die suddenly, will those closest to you know what to do? Will they know where your pertinent papers are kept or what assets may be available for your care?

While you are well and there are no health issues before you is a good time to begin to become organized. One area that is an absolute in this process is to have your estate planning up to date. At a minimum, you will need a will and financial power of attorney, which will appoint the proper people to handle your matters for you either during life or upon your death. A copy of these documents should be kept in a binder with your attorney's card on the inside. Make a list of all of your professionals who assist you such as your CPA, certified financial planner, life insurance agent, banker, physician and include the addresses and phone numbers for each such person. You should let the people appointed know the location of that binder so that it is available in the event that you need it.

In the event that you do not want to be kept alive by artificial means if your physician deems that you are in a terminal state, you should also have a living will and a power of attorney for health care, which should be kept in the same binder. A copy of the financial power of attorney, which contains the HIPAA language that allows your agent to access your medical information, the living will and the power of attorney for health care should be given to your principal physician just in case it is needed. If you travel, you should consider taking a copy of these documents with you, in case they are needed.

Another very helpful binder would be one that contained a list of every asset you own, including real estate, bank accounts, CD's, mutual funds, brokerage accounts, employee benefit plans, life insurance, safe deposit boxes, as well as a list of collectibles and other personal property. This will give the person who you appoint to take care of your interest while you are alive or the person that you appoint to wind up your estate a list of all of your assets, so that they will not have to search your entire residence and office to find them. This will also help to ensure that no asset is missed. Once a year, it would be a good idea to make a copy of the statements as of December 31st for each and every account, so that your agent will know the account numbers and the amounts that you have that can be used for your benefit.

Other documents that would be useful and should be kept in a binder would be your birth certificate, marriage license, divorce decree, military discharge papers, passport or green card, social security card, health insurance card, naturalization papers and copies of the car/truck/boat titles. These documents will allow your agent to apply for the proper benefits that you may be allowed.

Many people like to prepay their funeral expense. If you have, include these documents and a copy of the cemetery plot deed in your binder. Some people are particular as to the instructions that they have for their funerals. If you are one of them and want to dictate the church, clothing, if donations will be accepted, the get together for the family and friends afterwards, include your directions in your binder.

It sounds like a major project, but if you tackle it a little at a time, it will not be. Instead of leaving a mess for your family, you have made it easy on them at a difficult time for them and you can have your wishes fulfilled.

How organized are you?◆

14

Keeping Vacation Homes in the Family

As published in The Naperville Sun, September 2008

N ow that autumn has officially arrived, many people have spent fond memories of visits with their family in a vacation property. Perhaps you own a vacation property in Michigan along the water or at Eagle Ridge in Galena on the golf course. Wherever the property is located, one important question is how to keep the vacation home in the family after you have passed on.

All vacation homes require maintenance, from painting, sealcoating decks, replacing HVAC units, replacing roofs and on and on. If you have a number of children, how will they determine who will pay for these items? How will they decide which child can use the residence and when? Can your family even agree on decisions of this nature once you are gone?

One of the first things to do is to talk with your adult children about whether they wish to have the vacation home stay in the family. Many times you may assume that the children who enjoy the use of the home while you are there will want the responsibility of maintaining the residence and paying the real estate taxes and other expenses on the property. This may be an incorrect assumption, as your children may be raising their own children and have inadequate time or resources to even use the vacation residence. You may be surprised with the answers that you receive from your family.

If you find that your children do not want to keep the house in the family, you may wish to sell the property when the real estate market improves. If, however, you find that your children really enjoy the property and intend to use it with their families, then there are choices of what to do with the property. For instance, you can transfer your interest into a limited liability company, which will protect your family from a lawsuit if someone slips and falls on that property. It may also provide some level of asset protection.

If you decide to use the limited liability company, you should have rules in the form of an operating agreement that will indicate how decisions will be made with respect to the property, what to do in the event that the property requires maintenance, when additional funds may be needed for the property, when the property should be sold, who will be the manager of the property, to name a few. These are all important decisions that will hopefully keep the family from disputes when you are no longer around to settle such disputes.

In addition, in order to include your family in the limited liability company, you will need to make gifts of part of your interest in such company over time. Under current tax law, you may make gifts of $12,000 per person per year in ($24,000 if your spouse joins in the gift) before using some of your

Under 2014 tax law, you may make gifts of $14,000 per person ($28,000 if your spouse joins in the gift) before using some of your lifetime exemption amount.

lifetime exemption amount. You will need to consult with your tax professional or estate planning attorney to decide what is appropriate in the way of a gift to your family members.

There are a number of other ways to handle the transfer of the vacation residence to the next generation and keep it in the family, such as a qualified personal residence trust, a cost sharing arrangement or a partnership. Whatever way you may choose, it is best for you to be the one making the decision during your lifetime to minimize friction among your children about the use and care of this vacation residence.◆

15

Is Your Home a Good Safety Net for You when You are Older?

As published in The Naperville Sun, April 2008

S ince we are all living longer than medical science may have predicted when we were young, many times the principal assets an older person may have will be their home. Since most elderly want to stay in their own homes for the rest of their lives, if their physical health allows, many elderly are faced with a tough choice: either sell the home and move to an apartment or assisted care facility or make use of a reverse mortgage.

Reverse mortgages are a somewhat popular way for the elderly to make use of the equity in their homes. Many times bankers that they have always dealt with are eager to assist their elderly clients in obtaining the use of the equity in their home. If they do access the equity in the home, they argue, that senior should be able to earn more money on the cash, if it is properly invested, than the home as it may appreciate.

Just what is a reverse mortgage? In a reverse mortgage, the lender pays the borrower-homeowner money, which could be paid out to the homeowner as a

Reverse mortgages are a somewhat popular way for the elderly to make use of the equity in their homes.

lump sum, payment in monthly payments, a line of credit or a combination of methods. The home remains titled in the name of the owner subject to the lien that the lender places on the property for the amount paid out to the homeowner.   The owner is still responsible for maintaining the property, as well as the payment of insurance and real estate taxes on the home.   The homeowner does not make any payments generally on the mortgage, instead in many cases even the interest will be accrued.

This debt may actually increase over time, taking into account the amounts that the homeowner draws from time to time. After a period of time, there may be no more equity left in the home, as the amount of the draws may equal the value of the loan. There also may be times in which the amount of the loan may exceed the value of the property, which might occur at such a time when the real estate values are down. In that case, when the loan comes due, the homeowner will generally not owe more than what the home is worth.

One of the considerations about whether to use a reverse mortgage is a review of the fees. The fees for such a loan could be substantial—typically about 7% of the home's value. The fees are added to the loan balance generally and accrue interest over the period of the loan. All of these fees and the interest on them must be paid off when the loan is paid off. There are also closing costs that have an impact on the amount of the loan.

Another consideration is how much money is available to the homeowner from the loan. This is dependent upon the homeowner's age and the fair market value of the home. As a rule of thumb, an older client with a greater value in his or her home would receive more than a younger person with less equity in their home.

Another issue is that if the senior is using the proceeds received from a reverse mortgage to attempt to increase the earnings on this equity from the house, many times the yield on whatever the funds are invested in are less than the senior thought or have substantial penalties to draw the funds out until some years out.

Despite all of these issues, in some cases the reverse mortgage is the only way out for a senior who may have been caught by an adjustable rate type mortgage loan that adjusted above the means of the senior to pay the monthly payments. It may also be the only way for the senior to stay in his or her home for the rest of his or her life when the money runs out, even though it becomes difficult for the homeowner to leave any property to their heirs.◆

16

Geriatric Consultant can Help Families as Parents Age

As published in The Naperville Sun, June 2008

A s the population ages, and particularly, our parents age, it is appropriate and helpful to use the services of a geriatric consultant. There are a number of companies in existence at the present time that offer a large variety of services depending on your family's needs. These firms are part patient advocate and part mediators with the family when required.

For instance, on many occasions it is necessary to determine whether mom or dad are able to live independently in their own home. While you might determine that mom or dad are not able to live by themselves anymore, a geriatric consultant may be able to step in, talk with your parent, evaluate the parent's health as well as their home and surroundings. They also attempt to involve the parent in the decision which, at your parent's age, is a huge step for that parent to take. Most geriatric consultants began their careers in the nursing field and many have advanced training in dealing with elder depression, which affects many elderly people that may come as a result of poor nutrition, bad drug interactions or infirmities due to age. The geriatric consultants can also connect the family with the appropriate physicians or treatments for the senior parent based upon their evaluation of the issues.

Sometimes, it is appropriate to have that parent live in assisted care. Many times, however, with the addition of a part time care assistant, you must modify the home environment to include items in the home that would extend the time that the senior parent may be able to live in his or her own home semi independently. This may involve a structural change to the residence, such as an elevator or chair to allow the senior to go to the second floor, or a remodel of the first floor to accommodate another bedroom, or making sure that the proper on-site caretaker is there to assist with chores around the home.

The geriatric consultant can also help to mediate between siblings, many of whom may have a different idea of how to help their parent. One sibling may feel that the parent would be better off in a nursing home or assisted care, while another may determine that the parent should stay in his or her home. The senior parent normally has enough of their own fears to deal with and tend to react negatively towards the conflicts between their children over what will happen with their life.

If the parent has had extensive medical bills that need to be sorted or reimbursement needs to be applied for, many geriatric consultants may supply this need. They also can assist in finding an appropriate assisted care or nursing home facility that would accommodate your parent's needs and wishes. If your parent requires in home care, they can provide the personnel to do it, provide meals, escort your parent to medical appointments, supervised the on-site caretaker and provide many other services.

The bottom line is that using a geriatric consultant will give your family peace of mind, as many of my clients can attest to.◆

17

Parents of Special Needs Children Should Develop Plan for Later in Life

As published in The Naperville Sun, April 2007

If you have a child with special needs, you understandably worry about taking care of their needs while you are alive, but also after you have died. A disabled or special needs parent needs to find appropriate care and services, work with the child to obtain independent living skills to the extent possible and protect that child from any harm. This type of planning involves managing finances and making personal decisions in the event of the disability or death of both parents. A disabled child may need the parent to make decisions for that child well into adulthood and need to look forward to future residential needs, as well as finding the appropriate caretaker for that child when they are unable to do so.

First, one should note that without appropriate estate planning, the disabled or special needs child will inherit from the parents. Since the child is not able to manage the financial assets, this would most probably require the court appointment of a guardian. Such a guardian would have to request for distributions to be made for the benefit of the child and account to the court each year. In addition, if the child inherits from the parents, the assets that the child is entitled to receive may preclude the child from obtaining certain types of governmental assistance benefits without the assets being spent for their benefit prior to applying for governmental aid programs.

The goal is to insure that the child is not disqualified from receiving assets placed in the child's name at the parents' deaths or disability.

 The area of governmental benefit programs is complex, as the child may be entitled to one or more programs and the requirements are different for each type of program. For instance, unearned income and ownership of assets do not affect eligibility for Social Security and Medicare benefits (when the child is an older adult), but they do for Supplemental Security Income (SSI) and Medicaid. SSI eligibility is affected not only by cash and checks paid to a child but also by in-kind income in the form of goods and services purchased by third parties. The goal is to insure that the child is not disqualified from receiving assets placed in the child's name at the parents' death or disability.

Many parents make use of a discretionary special needs trust. This trust document is established and funded by the parents and must clearly state that the purpose of the trust is to supplement, not to replace, funds available from governmental and other benefit programs. The trustee must have complete discretion to use the funds in any way for the beneficiary. In addition, the child must not have any legal right to access the assets of the trust or the income of the trust. The trustee chosen must understand the rules concerning the governmental programs, so as to not make a distribution that will adversely impact the child's eligibility to obtain governmental assistance.

It may also be advisable to obtain a comprehensive professional evaluation of the child's physical, medical, social, emotional, education and services needs, if one has not yet been done. This will assist your attorney and financial advisor to refer you to the appropriate case manager or agencies that service children with the particular disability that the child has that will be the most beneficial to the child.

Caring for a disabled child or one with special needs is a 24/7 job. If you are no longer around to do this job, you should plan ahead to make sure that your child will obtain proper care and be able to live a life that will be the best under the circumstances.◆

18

Know the Rules before Listing Beneficiaries to IRA Account

As published in The Naperville Sun, January 2008

A s the baby boomers retire, they are the first generation that will retire with large IRA accounts. When the boomers do their estate planning, one of the considerations in such planning is who to name the beneficiary of the large IRA account. One consideration for such a choice is certainly to try to minimize the tax burden on their estates.

Most boomers do not realize that the money that they have saved in their employee benefit accounts or IRA accounts are subject to income taxes by the recipient, as well as estate taxes on the account upon the death of the

IRA owner. If both the estate of the IRA holder and the recipient of the balance of the account are in the maximum tax brackets for federal estate taxes and income taxes, the employee benefit account or IRA account could be taxed up to 85% of the total value of that account!

...the employee benefit account or IRA account could be taxed up to 85% of the total value of that account!

One option is to leave the IRA (or separate the IRA into several IRA accounts and leave one of the IRA accounts) directly to charity upon the death of the IRA holder. Under the current tax law, the estate should be entitled to a charitable tax deduction for the amount in the account.

In order to reduce or defer income tax and protect an IRA account from creditors after the owner's death, the best thing to do may be to leave the account to a trust. Since so many beneficiaries are targets of potential creditors from failed marriages to failed businesses to unpaid creditor issues, the IRA owner may well wish to protect the beneficiary from the loss of the IRA account to these creditors by leaving this IRA to a trust. With respect to reducing or further deferring income taxes on the account, the key is that an IRA trust must be structured such that the required distributions are stretched out over time, allowing a beneficiary to defer income taxes. The goal should be to spread the distributions over the life expectancy of the youngest beneficiary, which should allow for the longest deferral time.

The IRA owner can designate either a conduit trust or an accumulation trust as the "designated beneficiary" of the IRA account. A conduit trust automatically qualifies as a designated beneficiary under the IRS safe harbor provisions. If you have a beneficiary that has a gambling addiction or existing known creditors, a conduit trust may not be adequate to protect the beneficiary. Instead, your choice might be an accumulation trust, in which case you need to find an attorney who knows the rules, i.e. the trust must be valid under state law, be irrevocable upon death, have identifiable beneficiaries and be provided to the plan administrator by October 31 following the year of death.

The biggest problem is the beneficiary being identifiable. If any beneficiary of an accumulation trust is a charity, the trust cannot stretch out the distributions over time, as the IRS deems that charities do not have a life expectancy. If the named beneficiary holds a power of appointment under the trust, the trust also fails to qualify. It is more likely to have an accumulation trust qualify if the IRA is left to a stand alone accumulation trust which becomes irrevocable at the owner's death, preferably a trust for one beneficiary.

Leaving an IRA account to someone whom the owner wants to protect is a whole lot more than filling out a beneficiary designation form. It requires an estate planner with expertise in the complex rules that the IRS has concerning IRA account beneficiary designations.◆

19

Think Twice before Listing Minor as a Beneficiary on IRA

As published in The Naperville Sun, November 2006

M any people like to leave the beneficiary designation on their IRA accounts with the specific names of family members. For instance, a husband might list his spouse as the primary beneficiary and, if she does not survive him, the children are listed as the secondary beneficiary. If the children are minors, will this be an effective transfer?

There are several problems with listing minors as beneficiaries of your IRA accounts. First, in order to have the money paid out from the custodian, the custodian may require that a guardian be appointed by a probate court. If the parents of the minor are separated or divorced, the parties can fight over who should be guardian and who should control the funds. All of this can result in significant unintended fees to the minor's parents, who may have to pay the tab in order to have access to the account.

In the event that the custodian requires a guardian, once the guardian has the money, the guardian does not have unfettered access to use it for the benefit and care of the minor child.

...once minors attain the age of 18, they can take their inheritance and do whatever they wish with it.

Many probate courts will require that the guardian come into court to request access to the account. Without such access, it may be frozen until the minor attains the age of majority under the law.

Another problem is that once minors attain the age of 18, which is the age of majority in Illinois, they can take the money and do whatever they may wish with it. If Grandpa is leaving a $100,000 account for his grandchild, the 18-year-old may think spending it on a fast car would be more important than spending it on higher education.

A better way would be to designate a trust to receive the IRA proceeds. While a trust may cost more on the front end, it can give Grandpa the peace of mind that his wishes will be fulfilled. He can choose who will be trustee, what type of distributions can be made from the trust and when distributions of principal will be made to the beneficiary, as well as when Junior will receive final distribution from the trust.

The trust can either be designed as a conduit trust, whereby all the income will be paid to or for the child's benefit until a certain age; or accumulate some of the income. If the income is accumulated, however, it will be subject to higher tax rates than if it is distributed to the child, who is probably at a lower rate.

A small cost for peace of mind.◆

20

Life Insurance is a Good Safety Net, but Not for Everyone

As published in Dollars and Sense, The Naperville Sun,
September 2009

T he old adage is true that life insurance is not so much about life as about death. The only time that you or your family benefit from life insurance is at your death.

The trouble with life insurance is that it is often confusing to general consumers, about both basic questions such as when to buy it and when to skip it, or more complicated questions about how much coverage and which is the best policy for you.

The first question is when do you need life insurance?

You need life insurance under the following conditions (if you don't fall into one of the categories below, you probably don't need life insurance at this time, but remember to review your situation again from time to time when circumstances may change):

- You have dependent children. The loss of your income will most definitely affect your spouse's ability to remain in the family home with the children or provide the level of education that you would have provided for your children if you were still alive and working.

- You are married to a nonworking spouse. In this situation, your death will affect your spouse's ability to continue in the same life style, as going to work for the first time or going back to work after being out of the workplace will result in a lower paying job with a much diminished standard of living.

- You have a working spouse with an income substantially less that your income. Life insurance is appropriate here as your higher income has given you a lifestyle that your spouse could not afford alone.

- You have parents or special need siblings to care for and support.
- You still have a large mortgage remaining on your home. Having life insurance in this circumstance will allow your spouse to use the life insurance proceeds to pay off the mortgage, easing your spouse's financial burden after your death.
- You are using life insurance as an estate planning tool and wish to provide your family with the proceeds of life insurance that will restore to them the amount of your estate that was diminished by death taxes.

Another question to ask is how much insurance is enough? The proper amount of life insurance would allow your beneficiaries and their dependents to invest the proceeds of life insurance and draw down the earnings thereon and some capital over time to live on to make up for the loss of earnings that the deceased spouse would have provided.

There are several basic methods to determine the amount of the insurance that you may need.

The standard rule of thumb to estimate the amount of your life insurance needs is to estimate that you will need life insurance between five and ten times your annual salary net of taxes. If your net salary is $50,000 per year, you would have a minimum life insurance need of $250,000 and a maximum amount of $500,000. This method is fairly simplistic and does not take into account the specific needs you may have, such as the price of your children's education or the amount necessary for a special needs child.

The second method seeks to replace the amount of your income over a number of years. For instance, if you earned $50,000 per year and you wanted to make sure that income was available to your spouse for the next fifteen years, you would need $750,000 of life insurance. This method is fine, as long as there are no special needs to address and you have little in the way of financial assets already.

The third and most detailed method is to review the financial need. In this approach, you would take into account the various expenses that your income would otherwise pay, such as the family's annual living expenses, tuition for college and graduate education, mortgage or debt payoff and future retirement needs, as well as any special needs. This approach will require a little more thought and effort on your part to determine what expenses will be covered and what expenses are already covered by financial assets, such as college expenses that you have already taken care of through Section 529 plans and the like.

Life insurance is not for everyone, but there are many times that it is a necessary part of your financial planning for your family's future.◆

21

Convenience Account or Joint Account?

As published in The Gierach Law Firm Newsletter, April 2011

Many times our clients will add a name to their bank accounts, making the account a joint account. Sometimes that client wishes to have the person who was added to the account handle the account for the convenience of the client. It may be that the client is an elder person and wishes to have an adult child help to pay bills, reinvest the amounts in the account from time to time. This account would be considered a convenience account. It may also be that the client intended that the person that is added to the account is meant to receive the proceeds of the account at the death of the client, based upon the donative intent of the client. If the client's account is deemed to be a convenience account, the amount left in the account is added to the client's probate estate at his or her death, to be shared among all the beneficiaries of the estate. If, on the other hand, the account is deemed to be a joint account, it is payable to the other joint tenant at the death of the client and the other beneficiaries of the estate are entitled to no part of it.

Over the years, there was no way to distinguish whether a joint account was meant to be a convenience account or a true joint account. When a person opened the account, they may have checked the box as joint account, as there was no other choice offered. There was no statute to establish a convenience account either. Effective January 1, 2010, there was a change to the statute which established a convenience account designation. Now, any person who opens a joint account with another person, can choose to list the account as a convenience account. A person will probably have to request that the bank open the account this way, as many banks have yet to create a designation for convenience accounts to offer to their customers.

For instance, if an elder mother, who is competent to make decisions, opens an account with her daughter's name on the joint account, but fails to list it as a convenience account, as the bank fails to have the proper designation of "convenience account," it is important for the mother to have some other writing to establish what she intended by opening the account. Without any such writing, there is a presumption under the law that a gift to the daughter is intended at the death of the mother.

What happens if the other joint tenant writes out checks for their own expenses prior to the death of the person who opened the account? In such case, there is a presumption of fraud when that other person takes the money out of the account prior to the death of the person who opened the account. To overcome this presumption would require the person to show that the person who opened the account intended to make a gift to the other person at the time the account was opened or at the time that the second person's name was added to the account. This may be a written document prepared by an attorney or a gift tax return which established the gift.

In the above example, the elder mother may become incompetent and cannot state what she intended, thereby causing the other family members to demand of the daughter who wrote out checks for herself to prove that was their mother's intent and go to court to force that daughter to put the money back into the account for their mother's care.

I'll bet you never knew that opening a joint account could be so complicated!◆

22

Seniors—Planning Ahead is Key to Financial Stability

As published in The Naperville Sun, August 2006

R ecently, there was a case in the news of a Brooks Astor, a New York socialite, who is now 104 years old. Her grandson was in a heated battle to remove his dad as Mrs. Astor's caregiver. In court papers that were filed, the grandson accused his father of ignoring Mrs. Astor's health and personal needs and requested a friend of Mrs. Astor's be appointed as her guardian.

While we may not all be in Mrs. Astor's social or economic position, senior custody battles are being propelled by a number of demographic shifts. As the population ages and more people live longer, more seniors are likely to eventually lose their mental or physical capacity, leaving decisions over their finances and personal care to others. With divorce and second and third marriages leading to tension among children and stepfamilies, there is even more tension over the care of aging relatives.

...more seniors are likely to eventually lose their mental or physical capacity, leaving decisions over their finances and personal care to others.

The ensuing custody battles are driven many times by long-standing family rifts and the desire to control the family assets.

Today many family members live far away from each other, making it more difficult to monitor the condition and care of elderly relatives. Sometimes family members are not even aware of the needs of the elderly relatives or the current condition of their care. For all of these reasons, it is important to have seniors take proactive steps ahead of time to minimize the chances of guardianship proceedings or custody battles later.

In Illinois, a person who is of sound mind and memory may designate a person or a bank trust company to act as a guardian (and may designate successor guardians) in the event that he or she is found to be a disabled person by the courts in Illinois. The designation needs to be in a written document and signed in the same manner as a will. The court will determine if the appointment of the designated guardian will be in the best interests of the person at the time the court determines that the person is considered disabled under the law.

A person is considered disabled under the law if that person, because of mental deterioration or physical incapacity, is not able to manage his personal or financial needs.

There are several other steps that a senior should consider taking. First, the senior should have a current financial power of attorney in which the senior appoints a trustworthy agent, often a spouse, another family member, or an adviser, to make financial decisions if the senior becomes unable to make them.

The senior should also consider the use of a living trust. The senior transfers the title to all of their assets into that trust. The senior manages the trust until the senior is no longer able to do so, and is then succeeded by a successor trustee appointed by them in their trust document. In the event that the senior is again able to manage his financial affairs, the senior can again control and manage the trust.

The use of the financial power of attorney and living trusts which hold the title to all of the assets may preclude a fierce family battle later. In many circumstances, there will not be any need for a court appointed guardian. Instead, the trustee that was appointed by the disabled senior handles all of the financial matters for the disabled senior and the agent appointed by the financial power of attorney handles financial and other items that are not owned by the trust. In that case, all of the decisions have already been made by the senior before he or she is unable to do so.

Currently, few people plan ahead. The survey done by AARP in 2003, which reviewed 1,500 people age 45 and older, found that only 27 percent had created a financial power of attorney document. So, if you don't want to be like Mrs. Astor as a pawn in a custody battle, you had better plan ahead!◆

Appendix

Glossary Of Estate Planning Terms

The following glossary contains some of the more common terms related to estate planning. The definitions for these terms are provided by Denice Gierach.

In some instances, external sources were used to provide concise and accurate definitions of terms. These sources include Black's Law Dictionary, the Black's Law Dictionary Online, and The American Bar Association Online Glossary.

For a full list of the resources used throughout this book, see the Bibliography at the back of the book.

Administration – The process of handling the estate of a deceased person. It includes collecting assets, making an inventory and appraising those assets, paying and collecting debts, filing and paying estate taxes and income taxes, and distributing the remaining assets to the beneficiaries of the estate.

Administrator – A person appointed by the court to manage the assets and liabilities of someone who has died without a valid will (called an **intestate decedent**).

Attorney-in-Fact – A person designated and authorized to act as an agent through someone's power of attorney. The agent, under a power of attorney, can usually do anything that the principal can do for him or herself and, as a result, the agent can make decisions that are legally binding on the principal. See also **Power of Attorney.**

Beneficiary – A person who is designated to receive something from a legal arrangement or instrument, such as the income from a trust, the proceeds from an insurance policy, or a decedent's property as designated in their will.

Bypass trust – A trust into which a decedent's estate passes, so that the surviving heirs get a life estate in the trust rather than the property itself, in order to avoid estate taxes on an estate larger than the tax-credit-sheltered amount.

Charitable trust – A trust created to benefit a specific charity or the general public rather than a private individual or entity. These types of trusts are often eligible for favorable tax treatment.

Codicil – A supplement or addition to a will, not necessarily disposing of the entire estate but modifying, explaining, or otherwise qualifying the will in some way. It amends the terms of a will so that a complete rewriting of the will is not necessary.

Conservator – A person appointed by the court to manage the estate or affairs of another who is legally incapable of doing so. More generally, a guardian, protector, or preserver.

Decedent – An individual who has died.

Descendants – One who is descended from another; a person who proceeds from the body of another, such as a child, grandchild, etc., to the remotest degree. Descendants is a good term of description in a will, and includes all who proceed from the body of the person named.

Disclaimer –**1.** The refusal, waiver, or denial of an estate or right offered to a person. **2.** The disavowal, denial, or renunciation of an Interest, right, or property imputed to a person or alleged to be his. **3.** The declaration, or the instrument, by which such disclaimer is published.

Durable power of attorney – As a general rule, the authority granted under a power of attorney terminates at the time of the principal's incapacity or death. The durable power of attorney is a document that remains in effect even when the principal is incapacitated. This type of power of attorney allows the agent to make critical decisions at a time when the principal is unable to manage his or her financial, medical, or other affairs.

Estate administration – See **Administration.**

Estate planning – A process where you meet with a professional advisor to organize your assets, assess your wishes, and draft important documents to ensure that everything goes as you would like it to upon your death. The most commonly known core document associated with estate planning is the Last Will and Testament. See also **Will.**

Estate tax – A tax imposed on the estate of a decedent who transfers property by will or by intestate succession.

Executor – The person named in the will who will take care of the payment of all debts from the deceased person's assets, file all necessary tax returns, liquidate the assets and make distributions according to the instructions set forth in the will. May also be called a personal representative, or, if a female, an executrix.

Fiduciary – **1.** One who owes to another the duties of good faith, trust, confidence, and candor. For example, the corporate officer is a fiduciary to the shareholders. **2.** One who must exercise a high standard of care in managing another's money or property. *The beneficiary sued the fiduciary for investing in speculative securities.*

Gift tax – A tax imposed when property is voluntarily and gratuitously transferred. Under federal law, the gift tax is imposed on the donor.

Grantor – **1.** A person who conveys property to another. **2.** A person who makes a settlement of property, especially one who sets up a trust. The grantor is also sometimes referred to as the "settlor," the "trustor," or the "donor."

Grantor trust – A trust in which the settlor retains control over the trust property or its income to such an extent that the settlor is taxed on the trust's income.

Gross estate – The total value of a decedent's property subject to federal estate and gift taxes.

Guardian – An individual (or bank or trust company) appointed by a court to act for a minor or incapacitated person (the "ward"). The guardian takes control of the ward's assets, invests the assets, pays out the bills, and must report to the court, giving the court an accounting of what was done with the assets.

Guardianship: A court procedure in which a person is appointed to take care of you and your estate, in the event that you are incapacitated. The person appointed by the court is called a **guardian**.

Health care power of attorney – A document that allows a principal to designate an agent to make medical decisions, including end-of-life decisions, on the agent's behalf. This document indicates when the power of attorney for health care is to become effective, and can include considerations regarding the quality or length of life of the agent.

Illinois law provides that a person, or "**principal**," may designate an "agent" to make medical decisions, including end-of-life decisions, on his or her behalf. The instrument for appointing such an agent is known as a power of attorney for health care

Heir – A person who, under the laws of intestacy, is entitled to receive an intestate decedent's property, especially real property. Note, **Heir** and **Beneficiary** are not synonymous.

Income – The money or other form of payment that one receives, usually periodically, from employment, business, investments, royalties, gifts, and the like.

Intestate estate – A probate estate where the decedent died without leaving a valid will. The property owned by the decedent is distributed according to the state statutes, rather than to the persons that the decedent might have preferred.

Inventory – A detailed list of assets, especially those of a decedent or trust that is filed with the court.

Irrevocable trust – A trust set up by a settlor that cannot be altered, amended or revoked at a later date. From a tax perspective, unless the settlor retains certain powers or benefits, the income generated by the trust and distributed to a trust beneficiary is taxed to that beneficiary. Any undistributed or accumulated income is taxed to the trust itself.

Joint tenancy – A tenancy with two or more co-owners who take identical interests simultaneously by the same instrument and with the same right of possession. Joint tenants each have a right of survivorship to the other's share.

Life estate – An estate held only for the duration of a specified person's life, usually the possessor's. Most life estates (for example, created by a grant "to Jane for life") are beneficial interests under trusts, the corpus being personal property, not real property.

Life-Insurance trust –A trust consisting of one or more life-insurance policies payable to the trust when the insured dies.

Living will: A document that expresses an individual's desires regarding the use of extraordinary measures to extend his or her life when the individual's physician states that there is no reasonable chance of recovery.

Living trust – A trust that holds the legal title to property. This trust is normally revocable and may be changed by the settlor, and provides for the management of the trust and distributions of the trust during the lifetime of the settlor and thereafter, many times eliminating the need for guardianship or probate proceedings. Also called an *inter vivos* trust.

Marital deduction – A federal tax deduction allowed for lifetime and testamentary transfers from one spouse to another.

Medical Directive: An optional part of an estate plan that designates a person who will be making healthcare decisions for a person who is in a terminal state. Also referred to as an advanced directive or a durable power of attorney for healthcare.

No-Contest Clause – A testamentary provision stating that a named beneficiary forfeits any gift granted by the will if he or she challenges the will.

Operation of Law – The manner in which a right or a liability can be created for a party, regardless of that party's intent. More specifically, the way some assets will pass at your death, based on state law or the titling of the asset, rather than under the terms of your will.

Personal representative – An executor or administrator of a decedent's estate.

Per stirpes – Latin "by roots or stocks." A method of distributing property so that it is proportionally divided between beneficiaries according to their deceased ancestor's share. For example, if all children are living, each child would receive an equal share, but if a child is not living, that child's share would be divided equally among the deceased child's children.

Pour over will – A will giving money or property to an existing trust.

Power of appointment – A power conferred on a donee by will or deed to select and nominate one or more recipients of the donor's estate or income.

Power of attorney – A legal document in which a person (known as a principal) designates and authorizes another person to act as their agent, or attorney-in-fact, to make decisions on their behalf. The agent, under a power of attorney, can usually do anything that the principal can do for him or herself and, as a result, the agent can make decisions that are legally binding on the principal. See also **Health care power of attorney**

Principal – **1.** One who authorizes another to act on his or her behalf as an agent. **2.** The corpus of an estate or trust. **3.** The amount of a debt, investment, or other fund, not including interest or profits.

Private trust–A trust created for the financial benefit of one or more designated beneficiaries rather than for the public benefit.

Probate – A court proceeding that happens after a person dies, where necessary. In this proceeding, the will is proved to the satisfaction of the court to be a valid will, thereby eliminating challenges of fraud, testamentary capacity or duress. This provides some court supervision for the executor's actions in following the will.

Property – Any external thing over which the rights of possession, use, and enjoyment are exercised.

Prudent-person rule – In the law of trusts, the principle that a fiduciary must invest in only those securities that a reasonable person would buy.

Qualified domestic trust – A marital trust (referred to as a "QDOT") that allows a foreigner in the U.S. to get benefits from a spouse who is a U.S. citizen. The benefits can be from estates, pension and retirement plans and to receive medical treatment. Any taxes that become payable are deferred until all dividends have been paid.

Qualified terminable interest property – A testamentary trust established to transfer assets between spouses when one spouse dies. Under this trust, the assets (called the qualified-terminable-interest or QTIP) are considered part of the surviving spouse's estate and are therefore not subject to the estate tax on the decedent spouse's estate.

Remainder interest – A lingering or remainder interest in an estate or trust despite assets being distributed properly to all beneficiaries. A remainder interest may be created based on the future needs of an estate following the dissolution of a trust.

Residuary estate – The property remaining in a decedent's estate after all debts, expenses, and previous bequests and devises have been satisfied. Also called residue.

Revocable living trust – See **Living Trust.**

S corporation – A U.S. corporate structure where the income of the firm is passed to the stockholders in a proportion to their investment and taxed at rates of personal income tax.

Self-dealing – The act or an instance of a fiduciary's using another's property for his or her own benefit, such as benefiting from a financial transaction carried out on behalf of a trust or other entity.

Settlor – Term frequently used for one who establishes or settles a trust. Also called a donor, trustor, or **grantor**.

Special needs trust – A supplemental fund given to a person with a disability that does not jeopardize any government support payments. It is designed to allow him or her to be eligible for government financial aid by limiting the use of trust assets for purposes other than the beneficiary's basic care.

Spendthrift trust – A trust that prohibits the beneficiary from assigning his or her equitable interest and also prevents a creditor from attaching that interest.

Tangible property – Property that has physical form and characteristics, such as a car, clothing, or jewelry.

Tenancy by the entirety – A joint tenancy between husband and wife, arising when a single instrument conveys realty to the husband, which provides limited creditor protection.

Tenancy in common – A tenancy by two or more persons, in equal or unequal divided shares, who each have an equal right to possess the whole property but no right of survivorship.

Testamentary – Of or relating to a will or testament.

Testamentary trust – A trust that is created by a will and takes effect when the **settlor** (**testator**) dies.

Testator – A person who signs a will. If a female, may be referred to as the testatrix.

Trust – A legal entity created by a trust document that holds the assets for the benefit of the maker of the trust (the **settlor**) or other beneficiaries named by the settlor in the trust.

Trustee – One who, having legal title to property, holds it in trust for the benefit of another and owes a fiduciary duty to that beneficiary.

Unified credit – A tax credit against the federal unified transfer tax.

Uniform transfers to minors act – A uniform law providing for the transfer of property to a minor whereby a custodian acting in a fiduciary capacity can act on behalf of that minor by managing investments and applying the income from the property to the minor's support.

Virtual Representation doctrine– The principle that a judgment may bind a person who is not a party to the litigation if one of the parties is so closely aligned with the nonparty's interests that the nonparty has been adequately and effectively represented by the party in court. For example, a judgment in a case naming only the husband as a party can be binding on his wife as well.

Will – A written legal document, signed with the legal formalities that the statute requires, which sets forth the instructions for distribution of a person's assets after his or her death. It also names an executor.

About The Author

Denice Gierach has over thirty years of experience preparing estate plans for clients with substantial estates, including many business owners. She has also handled probate, trusts, trust administration, and estate administration for complex estates.

She is not only a lawyer, but also a CPA, and has a Master's Degree in Business from the Executive Master's Program at Northwestern University. Denice ensures that current and future tax implications are taken into account in every estate planning strategy she recommends to a client.

In addition, Denice also has more than thirty years of experience representing family owned businesses and privately held companies. She has acted as the general counsel to these companies, and gives business advice to small- to medium-sized family owned businesses. She also assists her clients by giving them strategies to grow their businesses, preserve their business culture among generations and resolve disputes among family members. Because of her estate planning background,

Denice also helps her business clients with their estate planning and business succession planning.

Denice has formerly owned and operated several businesses besides her own law firm, including a $30 million real estate development firm and a corrugated box manufacturing company. She sees things through a different lens, discerning the business issues first, prior to putting on the legal hat. Denice works with her clients as part of their business team, with the growth of her clients as her first priority. Because of this lens, she can think outside the box in seeking solutions to clients' problems and focus on finding ways to enhance the clients' growth.

Denice is admitted to practice in the State of Illinois and the State of Arizona. She is also admitted to practice before the Northern District of the United States, the U.S. Court of Appeals 7th Circuit, the U.S. Tax Court and the U.S. Supreme Court. She is a member of the Trial Bar for the Northern District of Illinois.

In addition to her professional experience, Denice believes strongly in working with charities in her local communities to impact those people and animals that are less fortunate. She is Treasurer and currently on the board of The DuPage Foundation, a local community foundation with assets in excess of $63 million. She is past president and past director for the Naperville Area Humane Society. She is also past Secretary and past director for the Heritage YMCA, located in the Naperville Area. She is a longstanding member of The Rotary Club of Naperville and is a member of Vistage.

Published Works—Estate Planning:

A New Federal Estate Tax Law—What Does it Mean?, *The Gierach Law Firm Newsletter*, February 2011

Look for Changes in the Estate Tax Laws in the Fourth Quarter of 2009, *The Gierach Law Firm Newsletter*, August 2009

Law in Limbo as Citizens Ride the Roller Coaster on Estate Tax, *The Naperville Sun*, August 2008

Is This a Good Time to Transfer Your Wealth to Your Children? *The Business Ledger*, 2009

Consider a Donor Advised Fund, *The Gierach Law Firm Newsletter*, 2009

Giving Something Back—A Wise Investment, "Law Talk," *The Business Ledger*, August 2009

'Tis the Season to Give Assets to Loved Ones, *The Naperville Sun*, November 2008

If You Plan to Contest the Will, it is Best to Refuse the Bequest, *The Gierach Law Firm Newsletter*, September 2009

Using a Trust to Provide for Long Term Care, *The Gierach Law Firm Newsletter*, June 2010

Planning for Long Term Care for Aging Parents, *The Beacon News*, July 2011

Talking with Your Elderly Parents About Lifestyle and Money, *The Gierach Law Firm Newsletter*, August 2011, in two parts

Parents Medicaid Application May Be Affected by Gifts to Kids, *The Naperville Sun*, February 2007

Use of Powers of Attorney for Your Children Who are Over 18, *The Gierach Law Firm Newsletter*, February 2007

What Happens to Your IRA or 401(k) When You Die?, *The Gierach Law Firm Newsletter*, June 2011

Are You an Innocent Spouse*?, The Gierach Law Firm Newsletter,* June 2011

Convenience Account or Joint Account?, *The Gierach Law Firm Newsletter,* April 2011

Is Your House in Order?, *The Beacon News*, April 2011

What to Look Forward to in Taxes for 2011, *The Beacon News*, February 2011

It's Time to do a Good Financial Plan, *The Gierach Law Firm Newsletter*, February 2011

No Generation Skipping Tax This Year, *The Business Ledger*, 2010

How the Law Compensates Family Caregivers, *The Naperville Sun*, July 2010

A Nursing Home is Taken to Task, *The Gierach Law Firm Newsletter*, January 2010

Some Medicare Recipients Will See a Rise in Premiums in 2010, *The Naperville Sun*, November 2009

Taking Care of Mom and Dad When They are Elderly, *The Business Ledger*, 2009

So You Have Entered Retirement—Now What?, "Law Talk," *The Business Ledger*, September 2009

Just in Case: Organize Your Life in a Simple Binder, *The Naperville Sun*, July 2008

Keeping Your Vacation Homes in the Family, *The Naperville Sun*, September 2008

Is Your Home a Good Safety Net for When You are Older?, *The Naperville Sun*, April 2008

Geriatric Consultant Can Help Families as Parents Age, *The Naperville Sun*, June 2008

Parents of Special Needs Children Should Develop a Plan for Later in Life, *The Naperville Sun*, April 2007

Seniors—Planning Ahead is Key to Financial Stability, *The Naperville Sun*, August 2006

Court Decisions Put New Wrinkles in Eminent Domain, *The Naperville Sun*, March 2007

Know the Rules Before Listing Beneficiaries to an IRA Account, *The Naperville Sun*, January 2008

Think Twice Before Listing a Minor as a Beneficiary on IRA, *The Naperville Sun*, November 2006

What Can You Do with an Inherited IRA?, April 2012

What Distribution Do You Have to Take From Your IRA in 2009?, *The Naperville Sun*, February 2009

Life Insurance is a Good Safety Net, but Not For Everyone, "Dollars and Sense," *The Naperville Sun*, September 2009

Life Lessons Remembered, *The Naperville Sun*, March 2011

We Want to be Your Resource, August 2010

Beware of Advertisements on Tax Reductions, *The Naperville Sun*, September 2009

What Kind of FDIC Coverage Do You Have?, *The Naperville Sun*, December 2008

Protect Your Pets When You Can No Longer Do It, *The Naperville Sun*, July 2006

Prenuptial Agreements—A Safety Net, *The Beacon News*, June 2006

When to Review Estate Plans, *The Naperville Sun*, March 2009

Ten Secrets You Don't Know about Estate Planning, Wills & Trusts

Seven Myths about Probate and Trust Administration

The Top Seven Frequently Asked Questions about Probate and Trust Disputes

Other Published Works:

There are numerous other published works, including business articles, as well as helpful videos and other resources available online. Visit www.GierachLawFirm.com for more information.

Bibliography

Below are some of the resources that were used in the writing of this book:

"Black's Law Dictionary Free Online Legal Dictionary 2nd Ed." The Law Dictionary. N.p., n.d. Web. 10 July 2015.

Garner, Bryan A., ed. Black's Law Dictionary: New Pocket Edition, Revised from A to Z. St. Paul: West, 1996. Print.

Gierach, Denice A. The Beacon News [Aurora]. Print.

Gierach, Denice A. The Daily Herald Business Ledger [Chicago]. Law Talk sec. Print.

Gierach, Denice A. The Daily Herald Business Ledger [Chicago]. Print.

Gierach, Denice A. The Naperville Sun [Naperville]. Dollars and Sense sec. Print.

Gierach, Denice A. The Naperville Sun [Naperville]. Print.

"Glossary of Estate Planning Terms." American Bar Association. N.p., n.d. Web. 10 July 2015.